Talk to God and Listen to the Casual Reply

Recent Books by
Mark G. Boyer

Nature Spirituality: Praying with Wind, Water, Earth, Fire

A Spirituality of Ageing

*Caroling through Advent and Christmas: Daily Reflections
with Familiar Hymns*

Weekday Saints: Reflections on Their Scriptures

Human Wholeness: A Spirituality of Relationship

The Liturgical Environment: What the Documents Say (third edition)

A Simple Systematic Mariology

Praying Your Way through Luke's Gospel and the Acts of the Apostles

Daybreaks: Daily Reflections for Advent and Christmas

Daybreaks: Daily Reflections for Lent and Easter

*An Abecedarian of Animal Spirit Guides: Spiritual Growth
through Reflections on Creatures*

*Overcome with Paschal Joy: Chanting through Lent
and Easter—Daily Reflections with Familiar Hymns*

Taking Leave of Your Home: Moving in the Peace of Christ

*An Abecedarian of Sacred Trees: Spiritual Growth through
Reflections on Woody Plants*

A Spirituality of Mission: Reflections for Holy Week and Easter

Divine Presence: Elements of Biblical Theophanies

Fruit of the Vine: A Biblical Spirituality of Wine

Names for Jesus: Reflections for Advent and Christmas

Talk to God and Listen to the Casual Reply

*Experiencing the Spirituality
of John Denver*

Mark G. Boyer

WIPF & STOCK · Eugene, Oregon

TALK TO GOD AND LISTEN TO THE CASUAL REPLY
Experiencing the Spirituality of John Denver

Wipf & Stock
An Imprint of Wipf and Stock Publishers
199 W. 8th Ave., Suite 3
Eugene, OR 97401

www.wipfandstock.com

PAPERBACK ISBN: 978-1-5326-3910-4
HARDCOVER ISBN: 978-1-5326-3911-1
EBOOK ISBN: 978-1-5326-3912-8

Manufactured in the U.S.A.

Dedicated to
William (Bill) and Kathleen (Kathy) Tembrock,
married for fifty years,
friends for over twenty-five years.

Contents

Introduction

H e was born Henry John Deutschendorf, Jr., on December 31, 1943, in Roswell, New Mexico. The general public knows him better as John Denver, trained architect, international performer, a man who sings about his experiences of living, and, in doing so, reveals his spirituality. "If someone asked me what I'm about, I'd say come listen to my concert," Denver says on the cover of his 1970 album, *Take Me to Tomorrow*. "My best auto-biography is the music I sing," he says.

Denver began his career as a folk artist with The Mitchell Trio with whom he released four albums from 1965 to 1974. These albums helped to establish his music career. Performing primarily with an acoustic guitar, RCA Records released Denver's album *Rhymes and Reasons* in 1969; this led to his success as a solo artist. In 1970 two more albums were released by RCA Records: *Take Me to Tomorrow* and *Whose Garden Was This*. The success of those two albums led to two more in 1971: *Poems, Prayers, and Promises* and *Aerie*.

From 1969 to 1997, Denver released twenty-three recorded albums in addition to four live albums, three Christmas albums, eight compilation albums, two collaborative albums, and multiple singles which, ultimately, made it on a record. The music styles consist of ballads, country/western, jazz, rock, bluegrass, and love songs. As early as 1982, his biography in his anthology stated: "John Denver's popularity encompasses a complete cross-section of the music-listening audience. He is probably the only artist who consistently registers strong response on the National Charts, the Country Music Charts, and the Easy Listening Charts.[1] Some of his music is neo-romantic, an attempt to capture in poetry and music the sights, sounds, tastes, touches, and smells of a lifetime of experiences.

On October 12, 1997, at the age of fifty-three, Denver died in Monterey Bay, California, in a solo airplane crash. While piloting a two-seat, light plane, its engine failed, and he plunged into the ocean. After his death, two more albums of his music were released along with six live albums, one Christmas album, and a dozen compilation albums. All of them demonstrate the appeal of this great performer.

Through the lyrics of his songs, Denver reveals his spirituality, that invisible force which motivates or inspires his personal spirit and gives insight and meaning to what he did and why he did it. Spirituality, for Denver, is that energy which fills the sails of his soul and propels him throughout his life.

In 1996, I published *"Seeking Grace with Every Step": The Spirituality of John Denver* (Springfield, MO: Leavenhouse Publications). The title of the book, *"Seeking Grace with Every Step,"* is from the song "Rocky Mountain High" on the album of the same name. While the song is a ballad about a twenty-seven-year-old man getting in touch with his spirit in the mountains, it is also a song about the force which inspires one's spirit—God, who is revealed through a lifetime of experiences. The subtitle, *The Spirituality of John Denver*, attempts to identify Denver's spirituality as a lifetime of seeking grace, seeking God, with every step at every time and in every place. Through the lyrics of his music, Denver shares with the listener how he did that. Only five hundred ninety-four copies of that signed and numbered

---

1. Denver, *Anthology*, 6.

book were ever printed. Over the past twenty years, I have been asked repeatedly to reprint that volume, which I have refused to do.

Instead of reprinting the previous book, I have decided to rewrite and publish this new book on John Denver. This book's title, *Talk to God and Listen to the Casual Reply: Experiencing the Spirituality of John Denver*, also comes from the song "Rocky Mountain High" and is also part of a line from it on Denver's 1972 album hit, *Rocky Mountain High*. I think this new title more aptly captures the spirit that animated John Denver for fifty-three years.

As stated in the first book, I do not consider Denver religious in the usual sense of the term, such as being devoted to a particular set of beliefs or belonging to a particular ecclesial denomination. However, anyone who can sing about talking to God and listening to the casual reply is certainly a spiritual person. Anyone who sings about seeking grace and Christ on the cross burning with desire—from "Stonehaven Sunset"—had some spiritual dimension to his life. This book is designed to guide the reader through an analysis of John Denver's spirituality, as it is gleaned and categorized according to major and minor themes which emerge from the lyrics of his songs.

In order to guide the reader of this book into an experience of Denver's spirituality, a Reflection section appears at the end of each chapter. The questions in the Reflection section are designed to help the reader connect to Denver's spirituality by exploring the themes in Denver's music in his or her own life. One's answers to the questions can be thought about for a time or written in a journal for later review. Since spirituality is a way of life, the reader is invited to enter into Denver's spirituality and examine ways he or she possibly may live it.

This work considers only the lyrics written by Denver alone or those written in collaboration with others. No lyrics written by others alone, even though Denver may have written the music or collaborated with others in writing the music, are considered. Since the lyrics of a song form a poem, they are often free in form and make use of poetic license. Therefore, ambiguities occur and are sometimes not easily understood. The author identifies these throughout this book.

A further problem exists in a book such as this. The music of a song is married to the lyrics. Every syllable of every word rests upon and flies only with the aid of a note. Since the reader cannot hear the supporting music in this written text, some important aspects of a song—such as tone, mood, and setting—are lost. Thus, I recommend listening to the John Denver repertoire, especially the songs mentioned in each chapter.

In order to avoid copyright issues with reprinting lyrics of Denver's songs, I have chosen not to quote them. Thus, a paraphrase or an interpretation is used in place of the original lyrics. In some places, I summarize lyrics, especially when several things are mentioned in subsequent lines of a song. Footnotes indicate to the reader the name of the song if it is not mentioned in the text. The Bibliography and Discography lists the songs used in this book and upon which album they appear. Because of the many collections of Denver's music, making some songs appear on multiple albums—such as "Rocky Mountain High" on *Rocky Mountain High, The Wildlife Concert, Earth Songs, An Evening with John Denver, and John Denver's Greatest Hits: Volume 1*—I have chosen only one album to reference the song title in the Bibliography and Discography. For more information consult the Album, Year of Release, and Songs by John Denver chart at the back of the book.

My hope is that the reader will enjoy this thematic analysis of John Denver's music and come to experience his spirituality.

Mark G. Boyer

October 12, 2017
Twentieth Anniversary of John Denver's Death

1

We Are Never Alone

The title for this first chapter comes from Denver's song "Autograph." The phrase appears in a number of songs, as will be seen later. It refers to the presence of God in the world. This divine presence, commonly referred to by Denver as faith, can be discerned through the quiet and through the earth and its elements.

Denver's idea echoes the same theme found in Psalm 139. The psalmist, speaking to God, sings:

> Where can I go from your spirit? Or where can I flee from your presence? If I ascend to heaven, you are there; if I make by bed in Sheol, you are there. If I take the wings of the morning, and settle at the farthest limits of the sea, even there your hand shall lead me, and your right hand shall hold me fast. If I say, "Surely the darkness shall cover me, and the light around me become night," even the darkness is not dark to you; for darkness is as light to you. (Ps 139:7–12)

Solitude

The quiet is very important to Denver. He considers the quiet life among the mountains in "Wrangell Mountain Song." Likewise, in "Annie's Other Song," he sings about riding his horse in the high country of the Rocky Mountains, in which he finds quiet and peace. He also sings about seeing the stars in the night sky because they know what is on his mind. The theme of finding solitude in the mountains is emphasized in his ballad "Rocky Mountain High." The man who was born in the summer of his twenty-seventh year walks in quiet solitude in the mountain forests and along the streams. He seeks grace in every step as he reflects upon the beauty surrounding him. It causes him to look deep within himself in order to capture the same serenity he finds in clear, blue mountain lakes. In the quiet stillness, Denver states that he can hear symphonies.[1] Sometimes, however, Denver discovers that it had been a long time since he had listened to the quiet. In "Eclipse," he sings about the long time it takes for serenity to come to him, even saying that he doesn't believe that he knows what it means anymore.

In "African Sunrise," Denver indicates that an hour a day of solitude is necessary. He sings about quiet contemplation that comes with the stillness of dawn and how it calms his mind. The first light of the morning is both a promise and sign of the quiet of the solitude that makes his heart exalt.

Faith

In "All of My Memories," Denver dreams of somewhere to build faith; in "Sweet Surrender," he is looking for something to believe in, and in "Aspenglow," a song about the town in which he lived, he sings about believing strongly. In his famous "Poems, Prayers, and Promises," Denver sings about the importance of talking about poems, prayers, promises, and the things that people believe in. Such faith must be strong, states Denver, in "What One Man Can Do." When a person must stand alone, it helps if someone stands beside him, but it is his spirit and his faith that must be strong. This idea is echoed in his ballad, "Matthew." Denver narrates that after his uncle, Matthew, lost a farm, his family, the wheat crop, and his home in a tornado he found the family Bible, which reminded him of his stone-solid faith. A person who is strong in faith can feel the faith of a dolphin's sigh says Denver in "Ancient Rhymes."

Maybe the best explanation of faith is found in "Higher Ground." In this song, Denver sings about people who live with things in which they do not believe. He states that they are giving up their lives for that which is less than it could be. Longing for a home, that is, a place of inspiration, may leave a person feeling like an empty nest inside. For those who give themselves to faith, however, a deeper spirituality is the result. These are the people who reach for the higher ground, trusting their feelings.

Of course, faith can be lost as well as found. In "Singing Skies and Dancing Waters," Denver asks the person whom he had hoped was waiting

1. "How Can I Leave You Again."

for him about faith that falters in another person. If his faith should falter to the degree that he forsakes the person and discovers that he has turned away, will the other still be there for him? He asks a similar question in "In My Heart." He asks the lonely, sad individual if he or she has lost purpose and the faith he or she had.

Faith leads Denver to sing about never being alone. In "On the Wings of a Dream," he sings about listening to the voices inside himself which guide him and lead him to proclaim that he is never alone. Echoing the theme of light and darkness found in John's Gospel (1:5) in the Christian Bible (New Testament), he sings about the life of light and holding on during the dark to the light of dawn. Then, having either God or Jesus in mind, but without giving an antecedent to the pronoun *he*, Denver declares that *he* is there with him, for *he* could never leave. Even though the singer fails to sing, the truth of the song remains. In "Autograph," Denver again sings about not being alone, even though there are times when he would like to be. And in "It's a Possibility," he sings, about knowing that no one is really alone; in "Love Is the Master," he acknowledges that he was never, ever alone.

Denver is explicit about who accompanies him in "It Amazes Me." He states that it is the Father who watches over all. Likewise, in "Joseph and Joe," Denver declares that the Father is with him. In the same song, Denver contrasts Joseph and Joe, the priest and the cowboy, and what each offers the other. He writes that Joseph, the priest, can offer God's forgiveness and help get one in touch with one's own spirit. Joe, the cowboy, who loves the desert and lives in the mountains, has but one close companion. Denver concludes that Joseph and Joe are really only aspects of the same person, who is cared for by the Father. Joseph may be lost in the city, and Joe may be lost in the desert, but there is something like a burning fire surrounding both the priest and cowboy. It is the sun, which reminds both that the Father is with them. And mother earth will teach both what each needs to learn about life.

Besides referring to God as Father, Denver uses the Hebrew Bible title Yahweh in "World Game." In "Druthers," he addresses the divinity directly as Lord. In "Two Shots," Denver sings about duck hunting and how if the Lord had meant him to kill a duck, he would have sent one in his direction! And in "Song of Wyoming," Denver sings about waking up on the range and, in a prayer, tells the Lord that he feels like an angel.

The divinity is simply referred to as God in "Sleepin' Alone." Denver sings that sleeping alone can make a person swear to God that the night will never end. Likewise, in "Daydream," he says that he wishes to God that a person were his again.

In *Anthology*, Denver provides a short, personal introduction to many of his songs. The song "Singing Skies and Dancing Waters" is "an expression of my faith in my father in heaven," he writes.[2] This clearly confirms that faith in God was important to Denver.

"Raven's Child" is Denver's only song to mention salvation explicitly. In the opening line he sings about raven's child chasing salvation. In Native American mythology, raven is an important animal serving as a messenger of the gods or as a creator god.[3] According to the song, raven's child needs to be saved from drugs, weapons, oil spills, and, especially, greed, which motivates the sale of drugs, weapons, and oil spills. Christians classify the abuse of these under the topic of sin. Denver is much more explicit. In "Stonehaven Sunset," he sings about the needs of many being the sins of a few and a future day when an accounting is due. In "It's a Possibility," he stresses the need to make sure that all injustice will one day cease. Denver calls this the day of sweet justice.

Salvation comes from God, says Denver in "Raven's Child." He sings about the true king, who sits on a heavenly throne, an obvious reference to God and Christ. That king is never absent. He lives in people's hearts. Thus, when people show compassion with wisdom and mercy, they reveal him to others. Even in a state of despair a tiny bit of mercy can free the soul of another.

Denver knows that people are more than they seem to be. "There is an ever-present regard for the state of man and the human condition" in his music.[4] He sings about peoples' potentials in "On the Wings of a Dream." He explains this in "Eagles and Horses (I'm Flying Again)" by contrasting eagles with horses as metaphors. The horses represent the body, which is tied to the earth. Horses gallop on the earth, living, dying, and giving birth. They run in their freedom. The eagles represent the soul. They demonstrate their freedom by flying without limit, seeing and hearing everything. Once the basic metaphors are established, Denver sings about the body being merely the shell of one's soul, yet the flesh must be given its due. The

---

2. Denver, *Anthology*, 281.

3. Boyer, *An Abecedarian of Animal Spirit Guides*, 122-131.

4. Denver, *Anthology*, 6.

purpose of the body is to carry the soul like a horse carries its rider back home. One's soul or spirit cannot be broken because it is free; it can rise up like an eagle with its wings. The whole song is set within the context of a vision of eagles and horses racing the wind and going higher and faster.

This song resembles some of the prophet Ezekiel's visions in the Hebrew Bible (Old Testament). More specifically, the prophet Jeremiah characterizes his people's enemy as having horses that are swifter than eagles (Jer 4:13). The prophet Isaiah characterizes those who wait for the LORD as renewing their strength and mounting up with wings like eagles (Isa 40:31). Both of those passages echo the LORD's words to Moses: "You have seen . . . how I bore you on eagles' wings and brought you to myself" (Exod 19:4).

One can't help but be reminded of another of Denver's songs, "The Eagle and the Hawk," which contains the same idea, especially in its opening line about the eagle that lives in the high country of the mountains, which Denver refers to as rocky cathedrals soaring into the sky. The soul is trying to get home to God. Denver makes this clear in "Higher Ground" when he sings about following his heart until it brings him home. In "The Eagle and the Hawk," Denver exhorts everyone to reach for the heavens. In "Downhill Stuff," he says that everyone is looking for heaven. And in "Alaska and Me," he says that there is nothing to lose and heaven to gain. The idea of getting back to heaven is one of Denver's ". . . Songs of the Way" in "Songs of . . . ," and thoroughly permeates "On the Wings of a Dream." In this later song, Denver states that life is just a path to the place from which all have come.

After reflecting on how people are never alone, as seen above, Denver brings together faith in God, the soul, and its desire to reach its heavenly home in "On the Wings of a Dream." He sings about the body passing away, but God, along with all other friends who have died, will receive people into the heavenly home. It is obvious that Denver believes that the spirits of those who have died continue to guide people from heaven. He makes this clear in "On the Wings of a Dream," when he sings about those who lead and protect others from the beginning of their lives to the end. Such guidance is a gift that God has given, and it can never be taken away.

Denver himself applies the song to his father, who had already died when he wrote this song. He would rather have him at his side, but he knows that his spirit is still with him. They are one, he says in "On the Wings of a Dream." The idea that the spirits of the dead live with people is also found in "African Sunrise." Denver sings about a lost son whose beautiful spirit still lingers.

Faith is also involved in Denver's theme of surrender. After asking about the highway to heaven in "Hold on Tightly," Denver says that a person has to hold tightly and let go lightly; surrender brings about forgiveness. He explains this in "Sweet Surrender," when he sings about surrendering to life and living without care. He compares such surrender to a fish in the water and a bird in the air. Just as the fish trusts the water and the bird is not concerned about the air, people must surrender to God—in whom they "live and move and have [their] being" (Acts 17:28a)—who will bring them to heaven. Christ on the cross burns with desire, sings Denver in "Stonehaven Sunset." The desire is that all people will believe and join him and his Father in heaven.

In the paragraph in *Anthology* which introduces "Calypso," Denver writes, "This is an example that I use when I tell people about being the instrument of that which wants to be written. Sometimes what you have to do is get yourself, your ego, out of the way and just let it happen."[5] Faith for Denver, it seems, is getting out of the way and permitting God to work within and through him. This process is commonly known as inspiration.

Prayer

Faith in God implies prayer, conversation with the divinity. Denver's songs mention the importance of prayer. In "Rocky Mountain High," he says that a person can talk to God and listen to the casual reply. In "Autograph," he exhorts listeners to say a prayer and open their hearts. Likewise, in "On the Wings of a Dream," he asks if the heart can find the way to God in a smile, a tear, a prayer, a sigh, or a song. In "Rhymes and Reasons," Denver states that the song is a prayer. The song he sings is a prayer that non-believers will join the faithful to find a better way in the world. And in "Poems, Prayers, and Promises," not only does the title indicate prayer, but Denver says that it is important to be with others and to talk about poems, prayers, and promises. Likewise, in "For You," he says that one of the things he values is just to offer a prayer each day.

Denver sings about wondering in deep contemplation, in "Whispering Jessie." And he states the importance of one person praying for another in "Back Home Again." He writes about a trucker who is only an hour away from riding on prayers in the sky.

5. Ibid., 191.

In four songs Denver actually sings his prayer. He asks the Father to hear his prayer of desperation in "Opposite Tables." Throughout the song-prayer he laments the confusion of his life and the fact that brothers are at opposite tables, like fire and water. In "It Amazes Me," Denver says a prayer of thanksgiving to God for creating the world. Twice he prays to God in gratitude for the way he made the world. The last stanza of "Higher Ground" is a four-line prayer. Denver asks that God keep him throughout the night, lead him to the light, teach him the magic of wonder, and give him spirit to fly. "Falling Leaves (The Refugees)" begins with a four-line prayer of thanksgiving to God. Denver thanks God for the day, for his gifts, and for love. He cannot help but break into praise.

Grace

No presentation of John Denver's faith and spirituality would be complete without a few words on his understanding of grace. In Christianity, grace is understood as God's free gift of himself to people. Grace is the action of God sharing himself with people. God makes the first move toward his creation; that move is to grace humankind with God's own life. It enables people to respond to God with a life modeled on Jesus, God's Son.

In "Rocky Mountain High," Denver's ballad about the changes that take place in a man's life when he moves to the mountains, he names one difference as a quiet approach to the high country in which the man seeks grace in every one of his steps. In this case, grace is manifested through the mountains, forests, streams, and lakes. Denver's "songs are celebrations of trees and flowers, the Rocky Mountains, blue skies . . . —all that is beautiful and good on this earth."[6] In "Rhymes and Reasons," Denver urges the hearer to seek grace in the way flowers bend in the wind without breaking. Likewise, in "Spirit," Denver says that a person who appreciates the wind is able to live with grace. The earth-made child of "Ancient Rhymes" is told that all of creation is drenched in grace, which is to be shared. When grace is shared, it gives hope to others.

In the second verse of "Flight (The Higher We Fly)," a song undoubtedly inspired by an airplane trip, Denver compares grace to flying. The last line of this verse is particularly revelatory, as he mentions touching the face of God. He begins by describing the blue sky into which he has soared with easy grace—places to which not even the eagle can fly. In a silent and solo

6. Ibid., 6.

7

flight into space, Denver states that he put out his hand and touched God's face.

Denver echoes 1 John 4:16, "God is love . . . ," in "Love Is the Master." Love is the master of everything that we do states Denver. 1 John says, ". . . Those who abide in love abide in God, and God abides in them" (1 John 4:16). Such is grace!

Spirit/Wind

While the Spirit, the third person of the Trinity, could be treated under the topic of grace, Denver's often mention of it indicates the need for a separate section. According to Denver, ". . . The spirit . . . lives eternally."[7]

There is a spirit that guides him, and there is a light that shines for him, he says in "Sweet Surrender." But the spirit also binds all together he says in "Islands." "The spirit . . . is in all of us. We are all one, we are all brothers and sisters, and it is that spirit which brought us into the world and that which will take us from this world to our home in heaven,"[8] writes Denver. This is why he can sing about how people are so much more in "Islands."

In "Cool an' Green an' Shady," Denver sings of each person's individual spirit. He presents a method of contemplation which begins with finding some grassy ground, lying down, closing one's eyes, finding or losing self—whatever is needed at the moment—and letting one's spirit fly! The same idea is expressed in "Higher Ground." In the last line of the last stanza, consisting of a four-line prayer, Denver petitions God to give him the spirit to fly.

In "Flying for Me," a song about NASA's former space shuttle, Challenger, Denver says that the crew's spirit was united to all people. The crew members gave their spirit to all.

According to Denver in "In My Heart," a person's spirit can be broken. He sings about the beautiful weather breaking his spirit. However, one's spirit can also be lifted, as in "Stonehaven Sunset." In that song, Denver says that his spirit is lifted, and it rises higher and higher.

Denver compares the individual spirit to a burning fire in "The Gold and Beyond." He sings about his spirit burning, consumed by the flame, to become one of the best in the world. This latter reference is an echo of Luke's description of Pentecost in the Acts of the Apostles. He writes about

7. Ibid., 193.
8. Ibid., 238.

the apostles being "all together in one place. And suddenly from heaven there came a sound like the rush of a violent wind, and it filled the entire house where they were sitting. Divided tongues, as of fire, appeared among them, and a tongue rested on each of them. All of them were filled with the Holy Spirit . . ." (Acts 2:1–4).

It is in the spirit[9] that Denver can say that he sings that he is flying again.[10] He sings to the spirit,[11] and he can hear Alaska's spirit calling him.[12]

Everyone and everything is permeated with the Spirit, just like everything and everyone experiences the wind. In fact, Denver uses the wind as a metaphor for the Spirit, just as did Luke in the passage from the Acts of the Apostles above. Also in John's Gospel, Jesus equates wind and Spirit, telling Nicodemus, "The wind blows where it chooses, and you hear the sound of it, but you do not know where it comes from or where it goes. So it is with everyone who is born of the Spirit" (John 3:8). On the album cover of *Windsong*, Denver writes:

> I wanted to record the songs that the wind makes, to play for you between the bands of this album, to share her music with you in the same way that I am able to share mine. In the many hours and days that we spent trying to record all that I hear in the wind, what I found was that you simply can't get it on tape. I hope that, at some time in your life, you'll be able to go someplace where it's quiet, where there are no cars, no dogs barking, no planes passing overhead, and that you will be able to listen to all of the music that she gives us. If you're really lucky, you'll be able to sit by a lake at the foot of a mountain and hear a storm come and go. There is beautiful, beautiful music there. All you have to do is listen.

The words of "Windsong" attempt to capture the essence of what Denver wrote on the album cover and can serve as a general outline of his understanding of wind as a metaphor for Spirit. It is important to notice the images which appear not only in this song, which seems to be the crystallization of all of Denver's understandings of the wind, but throughout Denver's music. He sings about the wind being the whisper of mother earth and the hand of father sky. He states that the wind sees suffering and pleasure.

---

9. "Singing Skies and Dancing Water."

10. "A Wild Heart Looking for a Home."

11. "Calypso."

12. "To the Wild Country."

Then, employing Greek and Roman mythology, he declares that the wind is the first goddess to learn how to fly.

The wind brings both bad and good tidings; the wind weaves both darkness and dawn; the wind brings the rain and builds rainbows. Indeed, according to Denver, the wind sang the first song ever heard. Referring to tornadoes, Denver states that wind is a twister displaying anger and warning, but it also brings the smell of freshly mowed hay. He compares a strong wind to a wild stallion race horse and the sweet taste of love in the summertime.

Just when the hearer thinks that Denver has exhausted the metaphors for the wind, he states that the wind sings in both cities and canyons and in both mountains and seas. The wind represents freedom. And so Denver's advice is for the listener to welcome the wind's wisdom. People should follow the wind's call both in their heart and in their spirit. By being immersed in the wind, people cannot help but join in her song.

Denver emphasizes his love for the wind and his understanding of the connection of grace, spirit, and wind in "Spirit." It is important to notice that this song appears on the same album as "Windsong." In these lyrics, Denver says to love the wind, to learn its song, in order to live with grace and be strong of will. The wind fills that empty space that exists in people's lives.

In "The Eagle and the Hawk," Denver exhorts the listener to dance with the west wind and to touch the mountain tops, to sail over the canyons and up to the stars. Similarly, in "Dancing with the Mountains," he states that he is one who dances in the wind, and all can be one when singing in the wind. In "Love Is Everywhere," Denver sings about the sound of the wind singing dreams for him. In "American Child," he asks the child if the wind ever calls in his dreams.

In a song about flying in an airplane, characterized as a spaceship over the mountains,[13] Denver brings together the image of the wind as something one flies through and which fills one's sails. He sings about riding on the steady breeze blowing strong behind him while passing through the clouds, like a sailor passes through the sea. "Trade Winds" makes this latter point more explicit. Denver sings about riding on the blue ocean and being propelled by a trade wind, which fills his sails with a pleasant breeze. Similarly, in "Flight (The Higher We Fly)," Denver sings about soaring in the sun's silence while chasing the shouting winds.

13. "How Can I Leave You Again."

While Denver believes that a person can taste the wind,[14] one can also feel the chill of the wind, which heralds snowfall on the mountain passes.[15] The wind can be cool and clean,[16] while it can also swallow the month of September.[17] However, Denver's favorite way of speaking about the wind is as a whisper. A whole medley is given to this image of the wind in "The Foxfire Suite: Whisper the Wind." Denver sings about the wind whispering over the water, through the night, through the canyon, and into the light of a new day. According to Denver, the wind calls all people brothers and sisters, and it tells them to love each other even as it whispers each person's name. In "For Baby (For Bobbie)," Denver states that the wind whispers one's name. While not explicitly using the word *wind* in "Song of Wyoming," Denver implies it, when he writes about the cottonwood trees in the canyon whispering a song about the state of Wyoming to him. Later in the same song he says that the wind in the sage brush sounds like heavenly songs to him.

In other Denver songs the wind represents freedom, as in free as a wind-swell in "Calypso" and as the old hitchhiker holding out his thumb in the wind in "Hitchhiker." The wind shuts the open door, and the wind still loves the songbird in "A Wild Heart Looking for Home." As a power beyond his control, Denver sings that he knows the wind can blow away everything in "It Amazes Me." And, finally, in "Wild Montana Skies," Denver exhorts the state of Montana to give the wild wind as a brother to the child in the song.

A synonym for wind is *breeze*. Denver compares a soft, baby's breath to a breeze which begins to whisper in "Season Suite: Summer." Also, in "Season Suite: Spring," he tells the listener to hear the breeze's message about the cold and gray being gone. In "It's About Time," Denver similarly exhorts that it is about time for people to start to listen to the voices in the wind.

The breezes in old Shanghai[18] are used as a metaphor for the voice of the person Denver loves heard in his ear. He sings about the Shanghai breezes being cool and clearing, like an evening's sweet caress. They are soft and gentle, reminding him of his love's tenderness. However, the pleasant-

14. "Season Suite: Spring."
15. "Love Is the Master."
16. "Sticky Summer Weather."
17. "Season Suite: Fall."
18. "Shanghai Breezes."

ness of the wind can be changed by the winter. In "Isabel," Denver portrays the woman in his dream as watching from the mountains for the first soft snows of winter and the icy winds they bring.

Thus, in Denver's spirituality, not only are solitude, faith, prayer, and grace important, but getting in touch with the wind enables a person to experience the Spirit of God.

Reflection

Denver sings about finding the divine presence in solitude, faith, prayer, grace, and spirit/wind. Where do you experience the presence of God? What name do you give to it? How do you describe it?

2

Our Mother Will Provide

The title for this chapter comes from Denver's song, "It Amazes Me." He says that while there are things in life that people must move through and there are some things they have to cast aside, the father watches over all while the mother provides for all needs. The father who watches over all is, as already seen above, God. The mother who provides is the earth. In Denver's spirituality, the earth and the other aspects of nature play an important role. After exploring the earth as mother, the other celestial bodies will be examined. This will be followed by a look at such features as mountains, forests, flowers, and water in Denver's songs. All these are elements of mother earth.

Mother Earth

In his songs, Denver often refers to "our beautiful mother Earth"[1] and as the earth who is the mother of all.[2] In "It's About Time," Denver says that people need to see that the earth is their only home, and that they face the fact that they cannot make a life alone on the earth. Mother earth provides, sings Denver in "It Amazes Me." In "Calypso," he says that to live on the land people must learn from the sea. Similarly, in "Joseph and Joe," he sings about mother earth teaching people what they need to learn.

In "Dancing with the Mountains," Denver asks his listeners if they were present the day the earth stood still. His question is in reference to

---

1. Denver, *Anthology*, 328.
2. "American Child."

Joshua's victory over the five Amorite kings at Gibeon. According to the Hebrew Bible (Old Testament) Book of Joshua,

> . . . Joshua spoke to the LORD; and he said in the sight of Israel, "Sun, stand still, at Gibeon, and Moon, in the valley of Aijalon!" And the sun stood still, and the moon stopped, until the nation took vengeance on their enemies. The sun stopped in mid-heaven; and did not hurry to set for about a whole day. There has been no day like it before or since, when the LORD heeded a human voice; for the LORD fought for Israel. (Josh 10:12–13ac, 14)

Denver, of course, has adjusted his song to refer to the earth standing still, based on contemporary cosmology, which understands that the earth revolves around the sun. The Book of Joshua reflects the previous theory that the sun revolved around the earth, still referred to in contemporary parlance as sunrise and sunset.

Because of Denver's love for the earth, he urges people to celebrate earth day every day in "Earth Day Every Day (Celebrate)." In this song, he refers to the earth as baby earth and wishes it a happy birthday. He sings about celebrating the land, the sea, and all the people who live on the earth.

Sun

One of the most frequently-mentioned elements in Denver's songs is the sun. He refers to it as sunshine, sunrise, sunset, and in other various ways. He sings about having seen a lot of sunshine in "Poems, Prayers, and Promises." In "Wrangle Mountain Song," he laments the fact that for seven days he hadn't seen the sun.

In "Aspenglow," Denver sings about seeing the sunlight through the pine trees. In "I Wish I Could Have Been There (Woodstock)," he expresses his wish that he could have been in the sunshine, listening to the laughter and the music. He says to look to the sun in "Joseph and Joe." "Goodbye Again" begins with Denver declaring that it is five o'clock in the morning and the sun is rising. No matter where people are, Denver says that it is the same sun in the sky.[3] Being in the mountains and singing songs for sunny days in one of Denver's favorite past times.[4] He also says that he would rather laugh with the rain and sunshine. In his "Rocky Mountain

---

3. "Shanghai Breezes."
4. "I'd Rather Be a Cowboy."

High" ballad, he says that the twenty-seven-year-old man who got his life straightened out in the mountains tried to touch the sun.

The best expression of his love for the sunrise is found in "African Sunrise." Denver addresses the African sunrise, calling upon the light to shine on the new day, to give people a new morning. It is the sun that enables people to stand on their own. Later in the same song he sings about the light being both a promise and a sign. For Denver the promise is one of a better way of life for Africans, and the sign that one day the hunger, caused by drought and experienced by so many people on that continent, will end. He demonstrates this very forcefully when he declares that the sun is what causes the seasons and brings the rain. Even though the people experience lots of dust, they keep on singing their way through the pain. One final image of sunrise in this song is that of the crowing cock, a traditional image of sunrise. Denver declares that he hears roosters crowing—music to his ears—and this experience leads him to pray for rain to wash away people's tears.

In "Anthem-Revelation," Denver urges the listener to see the sunrise, to open up his or her eyes. Then, after personifying *trouble*, he addresses it saying that he cannot see trouble when the sun is so bright. When it comes to sunset, in "Love Is Everywhere," Denver compares it to following one's heart like a flying stallion, and he urges the listener to race with the sun across the sky to the edge of the night.

He sometimes refers to the sunset as the sun slowly fading away in "Rhymes and Reasons," as the sun slowly fading away in the western sky in "Eclipse," and as scratching off sunsets in "All of My Memories." However, in "Eclipse" he explains that the sunset can refer to a person's lifetime. The sun slowly fading in the western sky represents not only a long day, but it represents an individual's lifetime coming to an end.

He begins "Song of Wyoming" with a similar four-line description of the sunset. At the end of the day, he is weary and tired from riding his horse. Meanwhile, night is coming. The sunset looks like there is fire in the sky, but the fading light brings about peace to the end of the day. The idea of the peaceful ending of the day is expressed in "I'd Rather Be a Cowboy." Denver says that he prefers to lie down at sundown in some starry field. Similarly, in "Trade Winds," he says that he never shivers when the sun goes down. In fact, in "Around and Around," he sings about loving to see the sun go down and the world continue to go around and around.

Just as he made "African Sunrise" his fullest expression of the daily event of sunrise, so he made "Stonehaven Sunset" function as a summary of his understandings of sunset. As he observes the sunset, he sings about it on the water, in the desert, in the city, and in the mountains. However, each day brings a new sunrise, too. He states that the sunset on the water looks like a burning fire. Likewise, a sunset in the desert looks like the desert is on fire. The sunset in a city can look like a city is on fire. And a sunset in the mountains can look like the mountains are on fire.

Sometimes Denver sings that his eyes cannot find the sun[5] and that the time might be just another lazy day looking for it.[6] He also says that at four o'clock in the morning he keeps tossing and turning while he is yearning for the sun to shine.[7]

Denver often uses the sun as a metaphor for various aspects of life. In "Sticky Summer Weather," Denver sings about the importance of dreaming of the future. Without plans for the future, life is not worth living; in fact, not having plans is like the sun hiding behind the clouds. In "Sunshine on My Shoulders," he sings about sunshine making him happy, making him cry, looking lovely on the water, and making him feel high.

He echoes the idea of sunshine making a person cry in "Back Home Again." He sings about sunshine making one's mother cry. In "Sunshine on My Shoulders," Denver again expresses how important the sun is to him. He sings about making a wish for sunshine all the time. When explaining how important another person is in his life in "The Gift You Are," Denver compares a person to a ray of shining sunshine.

In "Islands," Denver says that islands are stepping stones to the sun. He is referring to the morning sunshine streaking across the ocean and touching the islands, seemingly linking together all of them.

Because Denver believes that it is the sun that gives the seasons,[8] in "Season Suite: Winter," he says that during winter it is worth waiting for the chance to see the summer sun. He concludes this part of the suite by asking the sun to come and shine on him.

He begins "Season Suite: Spring" by exhorting the listener to open his or her eyes and see the brand new day with its clear, blue sky and bright, shining sun. This exuberance in the presence of the sun is an urge which

5. "To the Wild Country."
6. "Whiskey Basin Blues."
7. "Dreamland Express."
8. "African Sunrise."

is felt in the womb, says Denver. In "Ancient Rhymes," he writes about a precious earth-made child, who, before he or she was born, felt the urge of sunlight beams.

Another use of the sun as a metaphor is found in "The Gold and Beyond." In this song a race for the sun is taking place. Denver urges that everyone in the race realizes the equality of all people. Then, he sings about gathering in silence and singing for the sun.

Denver sings about the land of the midnight sun in "American Child," one of his songs about Alaska. In Alaska, known as the last great frontier, men and women can find freedom.

Moon

Along with the sun, Denver sings about the moon. In "Season Suite: Summer," he sings about the moonlight waiting for the dawn, and in "Love Is Everywhere," he refers to the moon as an old man who seems to sit on a white-top mountain. A similar reference to the moon is found in "Eclipse." In this song, the moon is in the eastern sky, hanging lazily among the clouds. Referring to the standard reference to the old man in the moon, Denver sings about seeing the old man smile and hearing him laugh.

In "It's About Time," Denver begins by singing about a full moon over India. This one is the same one seen in "Shanghai Breezes." It is also the one which heralds the birth of the precious earth-made child in "Ancient Rhymes." Denver begins this song by referring to the cycles of the moon. In "Annie's Other Song," Denver sings about the moon looking over his shoulder. In "Trade Winds," Denver dreams of islands upon which he wraps himself in the glow of a tropical moon.

It is difficult to tell in "Take Me Home, Country Roads" if Denver is referring to the moon or to a drink when he sings about a misty taste of moonshine. The dark and dusty road of the previous line of this song would hint at the former understanding, but the teardrop in his eye would indicate the latter interpretation.

There are two songs with references to the moon on the water. In "A Country Girl in Paris," Denver sings about the moonlight on the Seine, the river that runs through the heart of Paris. Likewise, in "Children of the Universe," he sings about the heritage given to all people, one part of which is to watch the moonlight fill the tides.

Stars and Sky

The sun and moon share the sky with the stars. Denver sings about both the stars and the sky. In "Stonehaven Sunset," Denver sings a song for the sky and for all the stars in it. In "Goodbye Again," he expresses the coming of the morning poetically by saying that the stars are fading quietly and the night is nearly gone. And in "Rocky Mountain High," he declares that the shadow from the starlight is softer than a lullaby, but immediately adds that he has seen fire raining in the sky, a reference to lightning.

In "Circus," he refers to the skies which look lazy, and in "Flight (The Higher We Fly)," he calls the sky the long, delirious, burning blue. In this song Denver also mentions the stars; he sings about how the darker the night is, the brighter the stars are.

Denver says that the skies are never still in "You're So Beautiful." A similar sentiment can be found in "Wild Montana Skies," a ballad. The very phrase "wild Montana skies" refers to the open plains of the state, usually referred to as "Big Sky Country."

In "I Wish I Could Have Been There (Woodstock)," he expresses his desire to have stood under the stars in the place where Woodstock was held. He wishes that he could have stood in the starlight with all the flower children. And in "Whispering Jessie," he sings about the warm nights of loving Jessie beneath the bright stars.

Specific star constellations are mentioned in "Spirit." Denver sings about Apollo, Orpheus, Andromeda, and Vega. He says that he learned how to rhyme the words in his songs from Apollo. He learned how to play them from Orpheus. Andromeda gave him a sign, and Vega lights his way. Also, in "Wrangell Mountain Song," Denver refers to the North Star. And, while not stars *per se*, in "Alaska and Me" Denver mentions the great Northern Lights of Alaska.

In "Flying for Me," the whole Milky Way is acknowledged. Denver sings about wanting to make a wish on the Milky Way and to dance upon a falling star. The stars become a metaphor for himself in "Dreamland Express." He tells the person with whom he is in love to let him be the stars up above. Similarly, he says to the person waiting for him that he would like to see her in singing skies in "Singing Skies and Dancing Waters."

In "Love Is the Master," the sky is used as an image of life. Denver sings about how a night in the wilderness is a magical thing; it is like seeing the brightness of the sky in the darkness. He uses the sky as an image of his life falling apart in "Come and Let Me Look in Your Eyes." He says that the sky is falling, and he is lost. He expands the idea to include the universe, stating that the stars are fading all across the universe. Thus, all people are lost.

Clouds

Denver also finds clouds in the sky. When attempting to put his life back together again, Denver uses the clouds as a metaphor. In "Come and Let Me Look in Your Eyes," he sings about the clouds sailing across the water; they will not let him see the sky. He applies this image to his life, stating that it is like his attempt to find himself. A similar reference is found in "Circus." Denver sings about the heavy clouds.

In order to emphasize how important a person is to him, in "The Gift You Are" Denver asks her to imagine a month of cloudy Sundays. Then, he compares her to the moment the sun came shining through, telling her that she is the ray of sunshine. A cloudy day can be cleared by the laughter of children and the loveliness of flowers in "Rhymes and Reasons," states Denver. However, the cloud named smog makes him despair. He sings about smog in "Eclipse." The heavy smog keeps him from seeing the mountains, and that makes him cry.

He mentions the fog in "Season Suite: Summer" when he sings about the silent morning mist lying on the water. But after climbing a mountain and seeing silver clouds below, a person can still have the Colorado Rocky Mountain high.[9]

Rainbow

However, there is also the rainbow. In "Rhymes and Reasons," the children and the flowers are like the colors of the rainbow. The rainbow metaphor is used in "Sticky Summer Weather" to explain the search for a meaning to life. Denver sings about looking for rainbows. He concludes the song by saying that he has spent a long time looking for rainbows.

The same sentiment is echoed in "How Can I Leave You Again." Denver says that he feels like his life is undone; it is like chasing rainbows in the setting sun.

The rainbow becomes a positive metaphor in "For Baby (For Bobbie)." Denver promises to sing the songs of the rainbow. Likewise, in "Dreamland

9. "Rocky Mountain High."

Express" he compares himself to the end of a rainbow. Later in the song he pleads with the person in his dream to let him be the end of her rainbow.

Storms and Lightning

Denver employs the image of a storm in "Back Home Again." He sets the stage for the song by singing about a storm coming across the valley and clouds rolling in. In "Annie's Song," he says that Annie fills up his senses like a storm in the desert; here he is referring to the freshness that surrounds the desert after a rainstorm. He capitalizes on the excitement of a storm at sea in "Calypso" when he writes about riding on the crest of the wild, raging storm.

Only in "Sticky Summer Weather" does Denver speak about the storm in a slightly negative sense, when he compares his thoughts to it. While reflecting on the thought of winter, he says that his memories rage like a storm.

He employs the metaphor of a storm in "How Can I Leave You Again." He says that while lost in a storm, he has gone blind. Here he is referring to a snow storm, which often leaves the person caught in it blinded for a time.

There are only two songs which mention lightning. In "Rocky Mountain High," Denver states he has seen fire raining in the sky. And in "Dancing with the Mountains," Denver asks about the night that lost the lightning.

Snow

The last element to be associated with the sky is snow. In "Two Shots," Denver sings about the sound of softly falling snow. Similarly, in "Aspenglow," he dreams of softly falling snow.

"Whiskey Basin Blues" sets the stage on a snow-covered night in eastern Wyoming. As has already been seen in the section on the spirit, the wind's chill reveals that there will be snow on the passes in "Love Is the Master."

In "Season Suite: Winter," Denver reveals that a lot of snow tends to make him feel down or depressed.

Mountains

There is probably no aspect of nature which is more important to Denver than the mountains. The mountain ranges across the globe have inspired him to write a number of songs. In the Rocky Mountains, Denver feels at home. After visiting Alaska's Wrangell Mountains for the first time, Denver said: "It was like I had lived there before. That's the first time I've been any place that felt as comfortable to me as the Rockies."[10] He wrote a song about this range—"Wrangell Mountain Song"—in which he expresses a desire to the see the Wrangell Mountains. In the same song Denver explains why he loves the mountains so much. He likes the quiet life in a cabin in the mountains. That quiet life produces gentle people. In another song about Alaska, "Alaska and Me," Denver says that he dreamed he was flying over the mountains and glaciers, and knew that he would live there one day.

In "I'd Rather Be a Cowboy (Lady's Chains)," Denver says that he would rather be camping in the mountains, singing songs for sunny days. He adds that he would prefer to live on a mountain than wander through the canyons of concrete and steel in the city. He characterizes himself as one who dances with the mountains in "Dancing with the Mountains." It gives him the feeling of being one with them. In "Poems, Prayers, and Promises," he expresses a wish to dance across the mountains on the moon.

There is something about the mountains rising right straight up to heaven, sings Denver in "Somethin' About." Also, he sings about leaving the city and being in the sun where the mountains make love to the sky in "All of My Memories." As far as Denver is concerned, it is only in the country where a person can hear the music of the mountains.[11] In the mountains, states Denver in "Sing Australia," he can hear Australia sing.

In "To the Wild Country," Denver sings about the spirit of Alaska calling him to the mountains, where he can find rest; to the rivers, where he can find strength; and to the forests, where he can find peace. He knows that he belongs in the wild country of the mountains.

The idea that the mountains share their spirit with people is found in "Stonehaven Sunset." When he sees lightning on the mountain, his spirit is lifted. This brings about a brotherhood between people and mountains, as Denver explains in "Rocky Mountain Suite (Cold Nights in Canada)." He sings about people and the mountains becoming brothers and sisters.

10. Denver, *Anthology*, 238.

11. "Rhymes and Reasons."

Such unity does not occur instantly, however. In Denver's ballad—
"Rocky Mountain High," about a man who came to the mountains to find
himself—he says that when he first came to the mountains his life was far
away. After he climbed cathedral mountains he began to understand what
life was all about and experienced the Colorado Rocky Mountain high.
Now, he knows that the Rockies are living and that they will never die.[12]

The same idea of the union between mountains and people is expressed in "Children of the Universe." Denver asks the listener if he or she
recognizes the life that lives within the silent hill. Similarly, in "Starwood in
Aspen," Denver says that his friends are the snow covered hills. In the same
song he refers to his home, named Starwood, as his sweet Rocky Mountain
paradise.

Denver finds the mountains to be a type of paradise because of their
unspoiled beauty. In the mountains, a person's senses are bombarded with
beauty. So, in "Annie's Song," Denver says that she fills up his senses like the
mountains in springtime.

In "The Foxfire Suite: Spring Is Alive," Denver mentions the Smoky
Mountains in the Carolinas. He says that life is good there. In his famous
"Take Me Home, Country Roads," he sings about the Blue Ridge Mountains, and says that life is old there, but it is younger than the mountains. He
summarizes all of his songs about the mountains in "Amazon (Let This Be
a Voice)," asking his listeners to let this song be a voice for the mountains.

Forests

Besides singing about the mountains, the rocky cathedrals that reach to
the sky,[13] Denver also mentions the forests, which can be found on moun-
tainsides. The forest, like the mountain, is a place of sensation. Annie fills
up his senses like a night in a forest, sings Denver in "Annie's Song." There
is something about the forest in the latter days of August muses Denver in
"Somethin' About."

The forest is even more exciting in spring. In "The Foxfire Suite:
Spring Is Alive," Denver sings about the life deep in the forest. In "American
Child," Denver understands the forest as home.

12. "Rocky Mountain Suite (Cold Nights in Canada)."
13. "The Eagle and the Hawk."

OUR MOTHER WILL PROVIDE

The spirit of Alaska leads Denver to view the forest as a place of peace in "To the Wild Country." He sings about hearing the spirit of the wild country calling him. In the forests of the wild country, he can find peace.

In his "For Baby (For Bobbie)" song, he personifies the forest as one who worships the person he loves. Leaves bow down when his lover walks by he says.

In his attempt at giving a voice to the forest,[14] Denver wrote "Amazon (Let This Be a Voice)," a song in which he reflects on how a single tree can represent the forest. He sings about a tree standing in the forest representing all forests. All trees in the forest are that one tree. In philosophical terms, the particular tree comes to represent the universal tree. Later in the song, he interprets the meaning of the tree for the listener. He says that it is the tree of temptation, a reference to the tree of the knowledge of good and evil found in the Hebrew Bible (Old Testament) Book of Genesis (3:1–7). He concludes the song by asking the listener to let this song be a voice for the forest. This idea is presented in a similar way in "Trade Winds." Denver says that the earth and everything on it sings to him.

Deserts, Canyons, Prairies

Like the forest, the desert appears in some of Denver's songs. There is something about the desert in the afterglow of evening he sings in "Somethin' About." What this something is appears in "Stonehaven Sunset." He says that the sunset makes the desert burn, like a fire.

After visiting Australia and writing "Sing Australia." Denver says that in the desert he can hear Australia sing. The listener must realize that the interior of Australia is mostly desert landscape. A person can hear Australia sing in the desert, like the mountains and the forests, because it is a place of quiet.

In "Rhymes and Reasons," Denver alludes to a passage from the Hebrew Bible (Old Testament) Book of the Prophet Isaiah when he sings about the children and the flowers leading people from the desert to the mountains by the hand and by the heart. With their innocence and trust, sings Denver, they will teach the meaning of freedom. In describing the rule of the new king of Israel, Isaiah paints a nursery room scene in which all the animals, who were previously enemies, live together in peace and harmony: "The wolf shall live with the lamb, the leopard shall lie down with

14. "Wild Montana Skies."

the kid, the calf and the lion and the fatling together, and a little child shall lead them" (Isa 11:6).

In "Somethin' About," Denver mentions two other of nature's phenomena: canyons and prairies. He muses that there is something about a canyon in the shade of a cottonwood tree, and there is something about a wheat field on the prairie. He concludes this song by stating that there is something about the land that makes him sing.

Flowers

While he never mentions specific flowers, Denver does use them in several songs in a generic sense. In "Rhymes and Reasons," he says that people must begin to seek the graceful way flowers bend in the wind in order to discover a way out of their confusion. The flowers are his sisters and his brothers, he says. They are both a promise of the future and a blessing for today.

In "American Child," Denver says that the flowers serve as the call of the wild to come home. In "Season Suite: Summer," he says that when all the flowers open up to gather in the sunshine, summer is present to stay. In "Season Suite: Spring," he urges the listeners to smell the sweet perfume of the flowers.

"Amazon (Let This Be a Voice)" presents more of a philosophical approach to flowers. Denver sings about a flower that blooms in the desert. One blossom of that flower represents all flowers, and all flowers are, indeed, found in that one. Later in the song, he says that the flower is a metaphor for faith. And he asks his listeners to let this be a voice for the flowers.

Water

John Denver uses the various sources of water on the earth to illustrate many of his songs. Water comes in the form of the oceans and the seas, lakes, the rivers and the streams, and rain. The morning mist lies quietly on the water he sings in "Season Suite: Summer." Yet, this quiet does not prohibit him from singing that he dances on the ocean.[15] In "Singing Skies and Dancing Waters," the dancing waters remind Denver of the person he loves. Nevertheless, he identifies himself as a sailor who runs to the sea in "How Can I Leave You Again."

15. "Dancing with the Mountains."

In "Islands," Denver refers to the water as the mighty blue ocean which keeps rolling on every shore, while in "Calypso," he simply calls it a crystal clear ocean, and in "Trade Winds," he call it the ocean blue. In "Annie's Song," he says that she fills up his senses like a sleepy blue ocean. And in "American Child," a song about Alaska, he calls it the icy blue sea.

Denver uses the auditory sense associated with the ocean in "Fly Away." He sings about life in a city making him yearn for the sounds of the sea crashing upon the sandy shore.

All of these references are best summarized in "Somethin' About." Denver sings that there is something about the ocean rising up to meet the shoreline that fascinates him. He also says that there is something about the water that makes him sing. In "Sing Australia," he adds that in the sea he can hear Australia sing. So, in "Stonehaven Sunset," he sings a song for the ocean. When the sun sets over it, it looks like the water is on fire.

Denver uses the ocean as a metaphor for travel in "Dreamland Express." He begins the song stating that he caught a ride on the Dreamland Express; it was like sailing on a blue ocean. In "Hold on Tightly," the ocean becomes a metaphor for being lost and confused. This song begins with being lost in a boat on the ocean, lost in a ship at sea, lost in the dark of misfortune, and not having a light to see. And in "Singing Skies and Dancing Waters," the turning of the seasons is compared to the tides of the sea.

Two songs speak about the light on the ocean. In "Sunshine on My Shoulders," Denver says that sunshine on the water looks lovely. Likewise, in "Trade Winds," comparing love to the ocean, he says that his love shines like the sea. Then, using the metaphor of an ocean wave, he says that he would like to take his love away on a wave in his arms.

Contrasted with his description of the ocean, a river for Denver is a place to go fishing.[16] But, he says that if he got his wish, he would prefer to go sailing, which he compares to camping on the sea. Yet in "American Child," Denver says that the rivers and the seas call the American child to come home to Alaska. Likewise, in "To the Wild Country," another song about Alaska, her spirit calls him to the rivers, where he can be strong. In "Alaska and Me," Denver says that he likes to sleep near and hear the sound of the slow, running river.

In "Rocky Mountain Suite (Cold Nights in Canada)," Denver personifies the mountain streams when he sings about the clear water laughing and

16. "Druthers."

singing to the sky. Likewise, in "All of My Memories," he refers to the sweet, singing river.

Watching the river roll along becomes a metaphor for just drifting and dreaming in "Song of Wyoming," as well as in "What's on Your Mind." In the latter song, Denver says that he likes catching a ride on a beautiful river because there is something about a river—that is, the way it runs to meet the sea—that entertains Denver[17] In "Amazon (Let This Be a Voice)," he explains his reflection as a river that runs from the mountains. That one river represents all the world's rivers, but all rivers are also manifest in that one. He says that it is the river of no regret. He ends the song asking his listeners to let this song be a voice for the river.

Like his philosophical meditation on a river, a lake can be a place of solitude and grace for Denver. In "Rocky Mountain High," a ballad about a twenty-seven-year-old man who comes to the mountains to change his life, Denver sings about the insight that occurs to the man when he experiences the serenity of a clear, blue mountain lake.

Just like he wonders about the oceans and the rivers, Denver also reflects on the rain. He says that there is something about a rainfall that makes it like the gift of living. Even if it is a drizzling rain, like that in "Alaska and Me," or if one has slept in the rain, as in "Poems, Prayers, and Promises," a walk in the rain is a sensate experience, as Denver explains in "Annie's Song."

In "I Can't Escape," a song about thinking of the one Denver loves, he says that every rain in the morning reminds him of his lover. The setting for the birth of the main character in "Wild Montana Skies" is in the early morning rain. In "African Sunrise," Denver prays for rain to wash away the people's tears, a reference to the hungry babies crying in Africa and the need to end a drought. In "Like a Sad Song," Denver says the rain is a song from heaven. It is the sound of heaven singing, and it becomes joyful music.

Animals/Wildlife

No presentation of Denver's view of nature would be complete without mentioning the role of domesticated animals and wildlife in his songs. Horses get mentioned more than any other animal. Denver's tribute to the horse is found in "Eagles and Horses (I'm Flying Again)." He begins by singing about horses as creatures who worship the earth, galloping on feet

17. "Somethin' About."

26

of ivory. They are constrained by the wonder of dying and birth even while they run free. In the second verse of the song Denver compares his body, which is merely the shell of his soul, to a pony that carries its rider (the soul) back home.

The four ponies on a long lonesome ride in Jasper, Alberta, Canada, are given credit in "Rocky Mountain Suite (Cold Nights in Canada)." In "Whispering Jessie," Denver says that he dreamed that he left his cabin in the mountains on an old palomino. In "Children of the Universe," he tells the palomino to lie back down and dream himself to sleep.

The horse and the palomino become a stallion in "Love Is Everywhere." Denver urges his listeners to follow their hearts like a flying stallion and to race with the sun to the edge of night. In "Windsong," he expresses the same idea when he says that the wind is a racer; it is like a wild stallion running.

Other animals which live on the earth mentioned by Denver include the coyote in "Song of Wyoming." the elephant, the lion with the sheep, and the grizzly bear in "Children of the Universe," and the polar bear in "American Child."

Denver mentions a large number of animals that live in the air, or spend a lot of their time flying. Prominent among these is the eagle. In "The Eagle and the Hawk," Denver assumes the perspective of the eagle and sings about the bird living in the high country, in what he names as rocky cathedrals reaching into the sky. What fascinates Denver about the eagle is the freedom he sees in the eagle's flight. He compares this to flying in an airplane in "Flight (The Higher We Fly)," singing about topping the windswept heights with easy grace where never the lark or even the eagle fly.

The fullest expression of the freedom seen in the eagle is found in "Eagles and Horses (I'm Flying Again)." Denver sings about the eagles inhabiting the heavenly heights where they are not limited or bound and where they serve as guardian angels of darkness and light, seeing all and hearing every sound.

Like eagles, hawks also give Denver a sense of freedom. The hawk flies with the morning dove, he says in "Children of the Universe." Assuming the persona of the hawk in "The Eagle and the Hawk," Denver sings about the hawk having blood on its feathers after it has killed prey. All who see the hawk soaring in the sky share in its freedom.

In five songs Denver refers to birds. In "Children of the Universe," he mentions the songbird. He sings about hearing the songbird's call. He uses the songbird as a metaphor for a person who is looking for love in "A Wild Heart Looking for Home." Denver sings that the songbird in a cage sings all day while watching other birds fly past its window. His wish is that the bird be set free to soar.

In the chorus of "For Baby (For Bobbie)," Denver says that little birds will sing along in time as all creation worships the person he loves. Similarly, in "Song of Wyoming," Denver says that he feels like he could sing like a bird in a tree. Earlier in the song he sings about night birds calling on the trail.

Denver's philosophical song, "Amazon (Let This Be a Voice)," collapses all of Denver's experiences of birds into one bird. He sings about a bird that sings in the jungle. That bird's song represents all music, yet all songs are summed in that one song. Denver identifies the song which the bird sings, saying that it is the song of life.

Other flying animals are mentioned in various songs. As seen above, the lark appears in "Flight (The Higher We Fly)." In "Children of the Universe," Denver contrasts the whippoorwill and the mourning dove with their natural enemies in the wild to indicate that all are children of the universe.

In "Earth Day Every Day (Celebrate)," Denver mentions the cry of a loon on a lake in the night. His inability to shoot ducks is the topic of the chorus of "Two Shots." He sings about taking two shots, hitting no ducks, and having only cold hands. And in "Wild Montana Skies," he sets the stage for this ballad by telling the listener that the wild geese over the water were heading north.

Besides the creatures on the earth and those who spend a lot of time in the air, Denver sings about those who live in the sea. His favorite sea animal is the dolphin, which appears in four of Denver's songs. In "Children of the Universe," Denver pictures the dolphin leaping out of the sea, as if engaged in a dance, twisting and singing to other dolphins. A similar allusion is made in question form in "I Want to Live." Denver asks the listener if he or she has ever watched dolphins frolic in the ocean's foam.

It is the dolphin which guides Calypso and its crew in "Calypso," while it is the muffled world of dolphin sound heard by the precious earth-made child in "Ancient Rhymes." In this latter song Denver employs the latest information available concerning the intelligence of the dolphin and tells the newborn child that the world holds to heart the dolphin kind, that he can feel the faith of a dolphin's sigh, and that he can sing the songs learned in dolphin lair.

The other sea animal about which Denver sings is the whale.[18] In "American Child," he uses the whale to paint the picture of the wild freedom of Alaska, the land of the midnight sun, where the whale swims in the icy blue sea. In "I Want to Live," Denver poses two questions to the listener. He asks if the listener has gazed on the ocean and seen the breaching of a whale. Then, he asks, if the listener has heard the song the humpback hears five hundred miles away, telling tales of ancient history, of passages, and home. For Denver, all animals of the earth, in the air, or in the ocean—including people—are one. By observing all creatures, people can learn some of the greater lessons about life, says Denver.

Respect for the Earth

Because of his faith and his great respect for nature and all creatures, in his spirituality Denver often laments the intrusion of people and their equipment into the wild country. In "Eclipse," he sings about people working with machines. And in "Rocky Mountain Suite (Cold Nights in Canada)," he says that the two men in the song are attempting to tell a story that should have been listened to earlier. Life in the mountains is living in danger, sings Denver. That danger comes from too many people trying to live in the mountains and from too many machines invading the mountains in order to create homes for the people who want to live there. This theme is also found in his ballad, "Rocky Mountain High." The man, who is now full of wonder, also knows fear. The fear comes from the attempt to tear down the mountains only to build other types of mountains. Thus, people scar the land.

In "American Child," Denver laments the introduction of machinery into Alaska's wilderness. He sings about machines changing the landscapes. Likewise, in "Eclipse," he literally cries when he sees the smog caused by machines in the mountains. Denver says that he worries about the ways and means of the world. He can see the future of the world killing him with its misbegotten highway of prophesies and dreams in "To the Wild Country." He continues to express the fact that people cannot live in the past, but when the loss is greater, a choice must be made.

18. "Children of the Universe."

In "Raven's Child," Denver confronts drugs, the arms trade, and oil spills. He says that raven's child's black beak has turned white from the crack and the snow. Concerning the arms trade, he says that nuclear warheads and lasers foster fear instead of simply choosing the right course of action. And his most searing attack is on the Exxon Valdez oil spill in 1989 on Bligh Reef in Prince William Sound, Alaska. He refers to the wing feathers of the birds blackened with tar and Prince William shoreline as being an unwanted highway of asphalt, an elegant scar on the landscape. Almost eleven million gallons of crude oil spilled into the ocean. Disasters are caused by greed, which, according to Denver, corrupts, makes a stone of, and silences hearts.

In "I Want to Live," Denver confronts hunger, killing, and wasting of life. He begs that there be no more hunger, no more killing, no more wasting life away. He also sings about global warming, stating that it is time to recognize the changes in the weather in "It's About Time." He expresses the urgency of taking care of nature, when he sings that it is time to see the earth as the only home people have and that it needs help. It is time to turn around the world, he sings.

This cry is echoed in "Trade Winds." Denver says that all the earth sings to him. In the conclusion of the song, he expresses what life would be like without the natural phenomena he loves. There would be no distant thunder, heavy seas, or Rocky Mountain memories.

In "Amazon (Let This Be a Voice)," he summarizes his cry for reverence for the earth. He asks his listeners to let his song be a voice for the mountains, the rivers, the forest, the flowers, the ocean, the desert, the children, and the dreamers. He implores his listeners to let his voice be one of no regret.

Denver can be this voice because he views the world as paradise. In "Starwood in Aspen," he calls his home a sweet Rocky Mountain paradise. And in "You're So Beautiful," he says that if paradise is everything one sees, the place one must be coming from is ecstasy. In the same song, he considers a place called paradise the spot where the person he loves was born. He says that each time he sees his lover, he is in paradise.

The same paradisiacal theme is echoed in "Like a Sad Song." When alone, without the company of the person he loves, Denver remembers that paradise was made for them. Denver's paradise is the earth and all the people who live on it. The earth deserves the respect and reverence of all. In

"World Game," he exhorts his listeners to use less of the world's resources and to do more to preserve them.

Denver put into practice both the using-less and doing-more aspects of caring for the earth. In 1976, he and Thomas Crum founded The Windstar Foundation, housed on a 1000-acre site near Aspen, Colorado. The goal of The Windstar Foundation was to create opportunities for people of all ages, from all walks of life, to acquire the awareness, knowledge, skills, experiences, and commitment to support a healthy and sustainable future—and to demonstrate that commitment through responsible action. The foundation emphasized service through research, communication, and education through its various programs, such as EarthPulse, Aspen Global Change Institute, The Windstar Biodome Project, Choices for the Future Symposia, The Windstar Award, Connection Groups, *World Watch* magazine, and International Work/Study Programs. Also, in 1992, John Denver founded PLANT-IT 2000, a foundation which focused on planting indigenous trees on public lands in the United States and in other locations around the world.

Located in Snowmass, Colorado, "Windstar [was] a research and education center devoted to developing workable models for scientific and technological progress which retain[ed] a sense of harmony among people working together, between mankind and the physical environment, and between . . . everyday concerns and . . . spirituality."[19] The foundation closed its doors in October 2012, sold its property in 2013, and donated the proceeds to an Aspen charity.

From this analysis of Denver's relationship with mother earth, it is easy to understand the importance of the sun, the moon, the stars and sky, clouds, the rainbow, storms and lightning, mountains, forests, deserts, canyons, prairies, flowers, water, animals/wildlife, and respect for the earth in his spirituality. All of the common, earthly things he experienced helped him become the authentic human being he was created to become. Through mother earth and all she contains, Denver partnered with the invisible spirit who also penetrated his life.

19. Denver, *Anthology*, 7.

Reflection

There are various elements to mother earth, according to Denver. Which one is your favorite? Why? In what ways does mother earth supply your needs? How do you show her your respect?

3

Can You Imagine One World?

The title for this chapter comes from Denver's "One World," which illustrates one of his primary values—the unity of all humankind. "When we think of each other, we are one with each other," says Denver.[1] Sometimes, however, "It's a world in constant conflict, with people working not for each other, but against each other, trying to separate themselves from each other—to make life not work."[2] For Denver what goes into this view of the world is a deep appreciation for the simplicity of life in the country, his home, wife, family, and all children, who represent the future. Indeed, Denver's songs "clearly indicate a concern for humanity."[3]

Country/City

Stemming from his reverence for all of nature and the inspiration it gives to him, Denver is opposed to life in the city and favors the simple life of the country. In "I'd Rather Be a Cowboy (Lady's Chains)," he contrasts the city life which Jessie—one of the characters in the song—chooses with the country life he chooses. He says that living on an L.A. freeway is not his kind of fun. He would prefer to live on a mountain side than wonder through the concrete and steel canyons of the city. The refrain of this song summarizes Denver's perspective on life in the city: He would prefer to be a cowboy and ride the range.

1. Denver, *Anthology*, 372.
2. Ibid., 25.
3. Ibid., 7.

In "How Can I Leave You Again," Denver echoes his sentiments about L.A. city life. He says that when he leaves his home for the city of angels, he feels like his life is undone.

He also emphasizes the contradiction of leaving the country for the city in the first two lines of the refrain of the same song. He declares that he must be out of his mind to leave the person he loves and head to the city. In "A Country Girl in Paris," Denver explicitly states that a country girl in Paris is a contradiction because she is dreaming about being in Nashville in the rain and thinking about a country boy who is now three thousand miles away.

"Country Love" further enhances the contrast between the country and the city. In the refrain Denver characterizes country love as kisses that occur in the kitchen, love that is honest and true, and being home with one's family. In the second verse, he continues lauding country love, comparing it to silky nights and warm, familiar hands. But he quickly adds that Nashville nights are lonely, but country love is not.

In "All of My Memories," Denver states that he is tired of big cities and their ways. It reminds him of walking in a maze. So, he prefers to leave city life—trash cans, bright lights, telephone lines—for the country and its sweet, singing river along with the sun on the mountains. In the country, he can build a faith, a farm, and a family. Denver says that he has wondered about towns and cities in "Song of Wyoming." In "Fly Away," he concludes that life in a city can make a person's ears hungry for the sound of the sea. Living in a multi-storied apartment complex can make a person long for things that he or she has not seen. The city makes one feel all closed in, says Denver in "A Wild Heart Looking for Home." Also, in this song he echoes the sentiment about city life making one crazy when he sings about nights in a city driving one insane with its frenetic activity and lack of quiet.

It's cold in the city says Denver in "I'm Sorry," but it always seems that way. In "Wild Montana Skies," a ballad about an orphaned boy who learns to be a Montana farmer, the man spends some time in the city and then returns to the country. Denver says that he couldn't breathe in the city, and he discovered that he preferred to live in the country.

Denver picks up the farming theme in "Let Us Begin (What Are We Making Weapons for?)." The song, set in 1943 western Oklahoma, describes a grassland farmer who is grateful to live in the land of the free. Four generations of farmers have worked the land, and not a single one of them ever gave up.

Denver does not want to live in New York City or Tokyo. In "One World," he states that he wants to live in his own village. This is because the cities start to crumble,[4] or they are filled with guns, poverty, and revolution. Denver calls this the streets of despair in "Raven's Child" because of the drug trade. In "Stonehaven Sunset," he sings about the city being on fire with guns.

In all of Denver's songs there is only one positive mention of the city. In "Annie's Other Song," he sings about having a wonderful time in a city. It is interesting to note that this song appears on no other album except the 1975 *An Evening with John Denver*.

Denver seems to concede that in his older years he will have to move to the city. "Whispering Jessie" contains a stanza about being an old cowboy from high Colorado who has become too old to ride and lives in the city away from the mountains. Being away from the mountains causes him sadness, says Denver. He says that he wrote "Eclipse" "about the sadness of being in the city for a long time, caught up in the smog and not being able to see the mountains."[5]

Picking up the theme of living in a cabin in the country, in "Wrangell Mountain Song," Denver sings about the quiet life in the mountains. In "Alaska and Me," after stating that when he was a child, he lived in the city, Denver says that he dreamed of Alaska. He would have preferred to have been born in a cabin there, even though it would have been a hard life.

It is not in the city where Denver's spirituality is fed; it is in the freedom of the country where he gives a voice to the wilderness and the land that he lives on.[6] Denver says, "I consider wilderness an invaluable resource that belongs to all the world regardless of which country or people or political elements is in control of the geography."[7] City ways make Denver want to hide, he says.[8]

4. "Rhymes and Reasons."
5. Denver, *Anthology*, 151.
6. "Wild Montana Skies."
7. Denver, *Anthology*, 281.
8. "Cool an' Green an' Shady."

Home

As has been seen above, Denver prefers the country to the city. His home, called "Starwood," is his sweet Rocky Mountain paradise.[9] "It's a beautiful place on the side of a mountain near Aspen, Colorado," he writes.[10] "The first time we [Annie, his first wife, and he] were there, we knew that it was our home."[11] However, he adds that home can be wherever one is. In "African Sunrise," Denver reflects this latter idea when he sings about an African sunrise smiling on his African home.

In "Take Me Home, Country Roads," he tells the country roads to take him home to the place where he belongs. He says that the radio reminds him of his home far away. He gets a feeling that he should have been home yesterday. He ends this famous song petitioning the country roads to take him home.

Denver says that there was a time that he didn't have a home. He writes: "I didn't have a place to call my own. I didn't have a room and clothes and records piled someplace."[12] It was on an occasion, after returning home "and feeling so good about being home," that Denver says, "I thought what it must be like for many people and tried to apply it to my situation and then say how wonderful it is to be back home again and experience all the things that you feel, the little things that represent home, that nothing out there on the road could replace."[13]

So, in "Back Home Again," he sings about how good it feels to be back home; even an old farm can feel like a long-lost friend. In this same song, Denver introduces a cliché which he uses in another song. He says that the little things, like a fire and supper, make a house a home. In "Sleepin' Alone," Denver says that neither all the tea in China nor all the glittering gold can make a house a home.

In "Wrangell Mountain Song," Denver sings about doing everything he can to get home. In "All of My Memories," he states that all of his dreams are of the place that he can call home. He characterizes this longing as a wild heart looking for home in the refrain to "A Wild Heart Looking for Home." This yearning for home permeates "Starwood in Aspen." Denver

9. "Starwood in Aspen."

10. Denver, *Anthology*, 76.

11. Ibid.

12. Ibid., 9.

13. Ibid., 150.

sings that it is always a long way home from wherever he is to Starwood in Aspen, Colorado. After being gone for a long time, it is easy to forget what it is like to be home at Starwood. Even in "Islands," Denver remembers his home in the high country. He sings about how the islands cause him to dream about his home.

Denver presents a long-way-home theme in "Prisoners." Speaking for prisoners, he expresses the wish to go home. In a number of repetitive lines, he adds that it is a long way home.

In "Annie's Other Song," Denver pictures himself as a gift which he is bringing home. He states that he is bringing himself—all he has to give in terms of life and love—home to the person he chooses to be with. Similarly, in "Circus," he begins by stating that he even looks like home. In "Daydream," he sings about the person he loves leaving and how he remembers all that they did together. Then, he begs the person to come home.

"Falling Leaves (The Refugees)" is a song about boat people who do not have a home. A similar song, "Hitchhiker," is about a man for whom Denver sings that the highway is the only home he knows. As the old hitchhiker continues to reflect on his life, he echoes words of those who tell him to settle down by building a home, but he knows in his heart that he will not do that.

Home is used as a metaphor in three of Denver's songs. In "American Child," Denver tells the American child that it is time to come home. Not only can this refer to coming home to Alaska, but, more importantly, to come back again to all that the American child has been.

Likewise, In "Sail Away Home," the lyrics about sailing away home refer to dreaming of a day when there will be no more guns. Denver concludes the song with the idea that the arms race is slowing down, when he sings about being on the way back home. Denver uses home to refer to finding the person he lost sight of. He says that his life became shady, he grew afraid, and he needed to find his way home.

There is no doubt that having spent a time or two in his own home is a value for John Denver.[14] So, he sings about finding his way back home.[15] In "Rocky Mountain High," home is used as a metaphor for the twenty-seven-year-old man finding himself. Denver sings that he was coming home to a place he'd never been before.

14. "Poems, Prayers, and Promises."
15. "Annie's Other Song."

Wife/Family

For Denver his home in the country is important because it is where his wife and family reside. In the music he wrote before he was married and had children, he expresses a longing for children and a wife. In "60 Second Song for a Bank, with the Phrase 'May We Help You Today?'" Denver sings about his dream of having children and a wife who would help him make a home. Likewise, in "All of My Memories," he dreams of somewhere to build a family. In "Poems, Prayers, and Promises," he again expresses the desire to raise a family. In his comments about "Poems, Prayers, and Promises," Denver says, "It's a song that comes from a very mellow space of family and friends; [it involves] sitting around enjoying each other and enjoying life in a way that has no time attached to it—no urgency and no frustration."[16]

After marrying and begetting children, referred to as having known his lady's pleasure in "Poems, Prayers, and Promises," Denver continues to express how much he values a wife and a family. In "Starwood in Aspen," when he is away from home, Denver says that he thinks about his lady's sweet memory and his children's sweet smiles. Likewise, in "Annie's Other Song," he tells his first wife, Annie, that she is his life, love, and the woman he chooses to be with. The last stanza expresses how she is always on his mind; even when he is alone, he is spending time with her in his thoughts.

Denver married Anne Martell of St. Peter, Minnesota, and they lived in Edina, Minnesota, from 1968 to 1971, when he purchased Starwood in Aspen. After he and Anne divorced in 1982, Denver married Australian actress Cassandra Delaney in 1988, but they separated in 1991 and divorced in 1993.

Throughout his personal life, Denver continued to sing about the importance of family, such as in "It Makes Me Giggle." In various verses Denver says that having a baby around makes him giggle and wiggle. Denver adds his amazement at his response to his son, who knows how to make him happy. After the adoption of his children, Denver wrote a song for his African-American son, Zachary John, and his daughter, Anna Kate. In "Zachary and Jennifer," he sings about naming him, raising him in the mountains, and swimming in the streams in the sun. He also sings about his daughter, who will dance in the wild flowers while singing in the summer thunderstorms. Besides his two adopted children, he also has a daughter, Jesse Belle, with Delaney.

16. Denver, *Anthology*, 54.

While not directly expressing his value of family, it is, nevertheless, found in a short song titled "Tools," a two-stanza piece about an abandoned baby rabbit who found a home in Denver's family. Denver sings about the rabbit, whose family left him behind, being his friend.

"Isabel," a song which is a dream about a woman hiding tantalizing treasures that the sun has never seen, represents the antithesis of Denver's wife/family values. When he sings about the moon as if it were a woman who wraps him in her arms, he knows that this mistress will betray him in the morning when the sun rises.

Denver's concept of family extends beyond those who live in the same house with him to the town in which he lives: Aspen, Colorado. "There's a sense of community and being with one another, having lived through some hard winter storms, cold nights on the mountain, thunderstorms, and brush fires," he says.[17] "Aspenglow," a song obviously inspired by Aspen, Colorado, Denver says, "is a sense of family, of living here, of being able to appreciate the little subtleties which are so often missed . . . ."[18]

Children

While Denver sings songs about his own children, he also sings songs about the smiling faces and laughing children who make a joyful sound,[19] and how they are a promise of the future and a blessing for today.[20] Denver says that their laughter and their loveliness can clear a cloudy day.

The theme of children, as the hope for the future, is one of Denver's strongest. He sings about seeking their wisdom.[21] In "Stonehaven Sunset," he refers to the child who is coming in the same line as dreams that come true. In "Let Us Begin (What Are We Making Weapons for?)," Denver connects fear for children and fear for the future. He sings about fear for his children, as he fears for the future.

"Alaska and Me" continues the future theme, but places it within the context of conservation of the earth. Denver salutes Alaska for all of the beauty his children will see. Likewise, "Flying for Me" extends the invitation

17. Ibid., 25.

18. Ibid.

19. "60 Second Song for a Bank, with the Phrase 'May We Help You Today?'"

20. "Rhymes and Reasons."

21. Ibid.

to make use of the earth wisely to all people. Denver sings that the promise for tomorrow is real for children of the earth.

In "Zachary and Jennifer," a song about his own adopted children, Denver expresses how children are like a mirror into which one can look with the hope to share the future. In the last stanza of the song, he sings about living on through his children and sharing their joys and sorrows.

All children around the world cannot be characterized as children playing[22] or as laughing children growing old.[23] Because of the sound of hungry babies crying,[24] in "Hey There, Mr. Lonely Heart," Denver advocates showing children that adults care about them by helping to remove their fear and hunger.

In "It's About Time," Denver begins a reflection on hungry children out of which he creates a whole song in "I Want to Live." In "It's About Time," his emphasis is both on the hunger of a man's child and the unity that exists between all fathers of children. While Denver does not know the man's name, his does know his home and family. There is a universality that Denver expresses in terms of feeling hurt when the unnamed man and his children are hungry. In "I Want to Live," Denver cries out for all children when he sings about their poverty. Assuming the voices of all hungry children, Denver sings that they want to live.

In the philosophical context of "Amazon (Let This Be a Voice)," Denver sings about a child crying in the ghetto. He says that that one child represents all children; all children are that one. Later in the song, he explains that the child is one of promise. He asks that this be a voice for the children. In "Stonehaven Sunset," Denver says that the children rise up and fall.

Denver believes that the children are the real leaders. By referring to the passage from the prophet Isaiah about "the calf and the lion . . . together," with "a little child" leading them (Isa 11:6), Denver sings about children leading adults by the hand and by the heart. Through their innocence and trusting, sings Denver, children can teach adults to be free. Furthermore, expressing universalism again, Denver claims children and flowers as his sisters and brothers. He expresses his belief that the spirit of children still lives in adults in "Thanks to You." "For all human beings, no matter who you are, the color of your skin, the philosophical, environmental, or

22. "Fly Away."
23. "Singing Skies and Dancing Water."
24. "African Sunrise."

religious heritage you evolve from, that birth cry of a newborn infant is the same," says Denver. "It is the absolute desire and demand to live."[25]

He continues: "Human rights are much more than just freedom of speech, freedom of press and religion. It is the right to breathe clean air; it is the right to drink and fill yourself, to cleanse yourself with clean water. It is a right that is denied millions of people today from before their birth. To me, this is the one obscenity in the world . . . ."[26] People need to celebrate living, according to Denver, the laughter that sings in the heart of a child. Children are the best teachers in Denver's spirituality.

All Are One

Another of Denver's themes is that of the unity of the whole. This aspect of his music is manifest in lyrics which express how all people are parts of the whole, how all people are brothers and sisters, and how all life is interconnected. In "Season Suite: Summer," he employs the metaphor of the world as a tapestry in which all can rejoice in their differences. And, yet, even though there is no one who is just like anyone else, all are, nevertheless, the same in some way. This leads Denver to conclude that he is a part of everything, and that a part of everything is in him. He says that the writing of this song "is an example of a whole lot of people working together to get one thing to happen."[27]

In "Rhymes and Reasons," Denver demonstrates this sense of unity when he sings about the children and the flowers who are his sisters and his brothers. He says: "I do not feel separate from any aspect or form of life. I feel part of it, and bound to it . . . . There is a brotherhood there, and a sisterhood."[28]

"Children of the Universe" is about the unity of all of creation. Denver sings about the dolphins in the cosmic ocean without bounds living in union with the whippoorwill, the grizzly bear, the elephant, and the whale. All of them, says Denver, are children of the universe; they weave together the universal tale.

Denver asks his listeners if their differences will divide them in "It Amazes Me." In "Downhill Stuff," a song about how some people like life

25. Denver, *Anthology*, 280.
26. Ibid.
27. Ibid., 89.
28. Ibid., 9.

slow and easy while others prefer the fast and breezy, Denver concludes that while each person has to do his or her own thing, all people are, nevertheless, united. He sings about everyone trying to get to that one point of unity through song. In "It's About Time," he sings that it is time for all to realize that everyone is in this world together. Later, in the same song, he says that it is time to start living this truth as the family of man.

"The world's survival depends on the sharing and dispersing of those riches in an equitable manner so that all people can benefit from them," says Denver.[29] Denver sings about this belief in "The Gold and Beyond." He says that in the mountain's eyes all people are equal. In people's eyes, one gets a glimpse of another's soul. When all struggle together, humanity realizes its unity. He concludes this song by saying that all gather together to face each other.

In "Hey There, Mr. Lonely Heart," Denver says that life could be so sweet and love could be so strong if all could be gathered as one family in which all the members shared all they had. In the deepest part of every human being, there is a sameness, says Denver. All that differs are the names. This idea is continued in "Let Us Begin (What Are We Making Weapons for?)" in a question. Denver asks about what it takes for people to learn to sing as a chorus. All that needs to be done is for people to imagine one world.[30] Denver says that the world is made for all, that each individual life is a gift for all others, and that if people realized this, then it could be one world.

Denver continues this theme in "It's a Possibility." Again, he moves away from the individual to the universal. He states that the fight is more than survival; it is for more than peace. If people just presented themselves to each other in trust, injustice would cease. While some hearts beat together as one, Denver advocates that all continue toward world unity. He concludes that one world made for everyone is a possibility.

Denver continues this theme of creating one world where all people live as brothers and sisters in "The Foxfire Suite: Whisper the Wind" and in "I Want to Live." He names the worker, the warrior, the lover, and the liar; the native and the wanderer; the maker, the user, the mother, and the son. All of them form one family standing together linked arm in arm, sings Denver. He explains it as a dance in "Dancing with the Mountains." After talking about how he dances with the mountains, the wind, and the ocean,

29. Ibid., 281.
30. "One World."

he says that his partners are more than pieces, more than friends. In the last stanza of the song he explains how dancing with the mountains, singing in the wind, and thinking of each other makes people one.

This transcendent aspect of unity, of making it part of one to be a part of another,[31] is worked out in more detail in "Flight (The Higher We Fly)," a song in which Denver uses the metaphor of flying to explain the experience of the transcendence of unity. In the chorus of the song he sings about flying higher and getting closer together. Similarly, "Flying for Me," a song written for and dedicated to the crew of Challenger, their families, and all the astronauts, staff, and personnel of NASA,[32] tries to capture the transcendent aspect of the unity of all through the metaphor of flight. Denver refers to a rocket as an arrow of fire that launches those in the space capsule into heaven. Later in the song, he says that being there would bring all one small step closer together. Those who flew in Challenger were flying for him and for everyone, sings Denver.

In "Amazon (Let This Be a Voice)," Denver philosophizes about the unity of all. He expresses it as seeing all in one. Thus, one river represents all rivers, and all rivers are that one. Similarly, one tree is all forests, and all trees are that one; one blossom is all flowers, and all flowers are that one; one song is all music, and all songs are that one; and one child is all children, and all children are that one.

He expresses the same idea in "The Foxfire Suite: You Are." In that song he says that he sees all of nature in one person, who is the morning sunrise, every rain, every peal of laughter, and every cry of pain. The song continues by declaring the one person to be all summer flowers, all falling leaves, everyone rejoicing, and everyone grieving. The third stanza declares that the one person is all unknown secrets, all hidden fears, all kisses of love, and all childhood tears. The last stanza declares the one to be the shining stars, the end of the rainbow, the reason a war is over, and the beginning of peace.

"Raven's Child," the victim of drugs, arms sales, and oil spills, is a constant companion, says Denver. Raven's child is the source of all sorrow and shame because, according to Denver, all people are one and cannot escape from the human race. Whatever one person does affects all people. After mentioning refugees in "Falling Leaves (The Refugees)," he declares that the refugees are one with all other people. Likewise, In "Stonehaven Sunset," he

31. "Follow Me."
32. "Take Me to Tomorrow," album cover.

states that all die together and yet somehow alone. What people should do, says Denver, is sing a song for each other.

With his understanding of the unity that exists in the universe, Denver sees every person as a potential friend. He sings about this in his ballad, "Matthew," a song about his uncle, who, after losing everything he had to a tornado, came to live with Denver, and, who, he says, came to be his friend. His "This Old Guitar" is a song about his guitar which introduced him to some friends. In "Goodbye Again," while he regrets having to leave, he sings about making new friends from people he does not yet know and who do not yet know him. Basically, he makes new friends, he says, through those who will listen to him sing. At concerts he frequently had to ask those in attendance to let him sing the verses of his songs and they could join in on the chorus! In "Starwood in Aspen," he addresses his listeners as new friends; he is happy to share his time with them.

In "What One Man Can Do," Denver says that people are more than friends. What they are, he says, are friends to all the universe and grandfather of the future. Denver is pained when brothers sit at opposite tables, like fire and water against each other.[33] He says that only a fool can't see the obvious ending. He is also hurt by the white man who took away the home of the red man. In "Wooden Indian," assuming the part of the red man, Denver sings, about being a wooden Indian with painted dreams inside his head. The eventual fate of Native Americans makes him wish that he were dead.

Such actions violate Denver's belief in the unity of all, an idea dating from the fifth century BCE and attributed to the philosopher Anaxagoras. He taught that people feel the spirituality of their existence when they have a sense of connection to things and the universe. In everything there is a portion of everything else. Denver's spirituality, illustrated by his songs, flows out of his understanding of the connectedness of all being. All are one, according to Denver.

Reflection

Where do you see the unity of all humankind demonstrated? With what other lives is your life connected? How can people's various differences be turned into unity?

33. "Opposite Tables."

4

I Live My Life in Celebration

The title for this chapter comes from John Denver's "Anthem-Revelation." In it he says that he lives his life in celebration that he has a life to live. The greater part of Denver's songs center on the various aspects of living—birth, growing up, getting older, and dying—and on the metaphors he uses to describe life, such as a journey. Through his music, he says that life is about changes, love, loneliness, memories, and much more. This chapter explores the elements that go into making a life for John Denver.

One of his most famous metaphors for life is "This Old Guitar." The instrument functions as a teacher of song, laughter, and tears. It has introduced Denver to other people and accompanied him in his loneliness, as well as being the means to meet his lady. It serves as the instrument for his livelihood. Life is summarized in this song. Denver says that the instrument taught him to sing a love song and how to laugh and cry. It was the medium for introducing him to new friends, to brighten some of his days, and help him through cold and lonely nights. In the second stanza the guitar gives him his lady, and it opens her eyes and ears to him. It brought the two of them together and enabled them to be themselves. In the third stanza, Denver sings about how the guitar provided his living and all that he loves to do, especially sing to the stars in the mountains and sing songs for those new friends who have gathered around him.

Birth

The celebration of life begins before birth, when one can feel the baby move.[1] Then, birth into the physical world takes place. In "Ancient Rhymes," Denver devotes a whole stanza to describing birth. He sings about how the child in the womb learns life's ancient rhymes for nine months before being born. Professing a belief in re-incarnation, every new birth is a soul regained, he says in "Love Is Everywhere."

Birth is not limited to one's physical birth in Denver's music. "Rocky Mountain High," the ballad about a man who discovers the meaning of life in the mountains, begins with the statement that he was born in the summer of his twenty-seventh year. Two lines later, Denver sings about him being born again. In "Love Is the Master," he states that every day is the day that life begins all over again. Likewise, the changing from winter to spring can be described as the rebirth of the earth. In "Season Suite: Spring," Denver says that the earth is reborn, and life goes on.

Journey

Once birth has taken place, the pilgrimage has begun. For Denver the best metaphor for a lifetime is journey. "Hitchhiker" tries to capture the essence of a lifetime journey. Speaking for an old hitchhiker, Denver sings about the highway being the only home he knows with no destination in mind; wherever he ends up is where he wants to be. Later he sings about the curiosity of wondering about what may be waiting around the bend in the road. He doesn't know what he may see. The hitchhiker says that he was only seventeen when he took the open highway, which became his teacher and friend.

However, this song also emphasizes the traveling status of the listener, too. In the opening line, Denver exhorts his listeners, who may be driving down a road, to pick up the hitchhiker they may come across. Because he has been a pilgrim all his life, the hitchhiker can tell about all the crazy things he has seen.

Denver invites his listeners to come and listen to the story of a journey once begun in "It Amazes Me," a song about a person's search for a way to serve others. He says that paths often come together, and those crossing paths have to ask about where they go now. Some things must be moved through, he sings, while others need to be cast away.

1. "Back Home Again."

In "Looking for Space," Denver calls his journey the road of experience. He says that through experience people try to find their way even as they live every day. This road of experience can be one upon which a person has traveled before. In "True Love Takes Time," Denver says that he travels down the road and searches the empty sky like others before him. He concludes the song by stating that all people travel the road of experience; some of them have been fools.

That road can be true love. In "Love Is the Master," the road becomes a trail to self-discovery. Denver sings about taking a journey to find himself while walking a trail, which ultimately leads him back home to himself.

The road of experience becomes a forgotten highway in "Sweet Surrender." Denver begins the song declaring that he was lost and alone on a forgotten highway which was traveled by many but remembered by few. In the second verse he expresses the openness, or sweet surrender, which needs to exist when a person is journeying through life. He says that there is nothing behind him and nothing that ties him to yesterday. Only the future, tomorrow, is open. Therefore, the best place to be is in the moment of awareness. He adds that he cannot know the future or where he is going, but there is a spirit that guides him like a light. This makes his life worth living

There is a dimension of exploration to one's lifetime journey. Denver captures this in a question in "American Child," a song about the freedom of the wilderness in Alaska. He invites the listener to imagine the primitive days of the forty-ninth state when an explorer had to make his or her own way through the land. The same sense of exploration can be found flying in a spaceship over the mountains in "How Can I Leave You Again." While he is looking out of the window of his airplane, Denver observes the pathways winding below him and remembers the times he has traveled over them. Similarly, the twenty-seven-year-old man in "Rocky Mountain High" is filled with adventure as he experiences his new birth in the Rockies. Denver says that when the young man first came to the mountains, his life was elsewhere—on the road—hanging by a song. He's been changed by his journey.

In "Joseph and Joe," a song about a priest (Joseph) and a cowboy (Joe) who travel two different roads, which in many ways are similar paths, Denver philosophically reflects on a life's journey. He sings about not knowing where to go next. He asks about knowing where the next part of the journey will take him. Hidden in the lyrics is a passage from the Hebrew Bible (Old Testament) Book of Ruth. Ruth, a Moabite, and her mother-in-law, Naomi, a Jewess, decide to journey to Bethlehem after the death of Naomi's husband and sons. Naomi tells Ruth to go back to her own people. However, Ruth says, "Where you go, I will go; where you lodge, I will lodge; your people shall be my people, and your God my God. Where you die, I will die . . ." (Ruth 1:16b–17a).

In "Starwood in Aspen," the journey involves a great distance. It's a long way from Los Angeles, California, to Denver, Colorado, Denver sings. But no matter how far away a person is, the journey of a lifetime continues. Distances are meaningless, says Denver in "Heart to Heart." They are like hands that move around a clock.

Questions and Answers

As a person makes his or her journey down the road of life, there are many questions and, hopefully, answers that come his or her way. Denver sings about searching for the answers to questions. He says, "When I look around me, in search of answers to my questions about life, in moving, and growing, and discovering, I find that I am really amazed. I can't believe how magnificent people can be, and how inhumane at times."[2]

In "In My Heart," Denver echoes this idea when he sings about life being a question he does not understand. Sometimes in the search for answers to questions a person can feel that he or she is looking everywhere, but going nowhere.[3] At other times, as in the case of the crew of Calypso, people are in search of the answers to questions yet unknown.[4] The most deadly place to be, states Denver in "Singing Skies and Dancing Waters," is to say that one has the answers to all of his or her questions.

In many of Denver's songs the answer to the question is love. "Hey There, Mr. Lonely Heart" begins with a question about love. He refers to the mystery of life's most precious seed as a touch, kiss, or need. He states that the gift of true love, a gift that is in the giving, is the mystery of life. "Heart to Heart" says that the answer to suffering is true love, which is always safe.

Denver says that he prayed that he would find an answer in the stars so that he could give a voice to all of the hearts that cannot be heard in "Flying for Me." In "Hold on Tightly," he sings about the heart, in which freedom, peace, and the answers to even deeper questions are found. In the final

2. Denver, *Anthology*, 281.
3. "Circus."
4. "Calypso."

analysis, the question may not have an answer, says Denver in "Looking for Space." It just may be that way.

Living

The purpose of life is living. Denver says, "Life fills me."[5] On the *Back Home Again* album cover he writes: "My purpose in performing is to communicate the joy I experience in living. It is the aliveness already within you that my music is intended to reach." In "Earth Day Every Day (Celebrate)," Denver says to celebrate living. In "Hey There, Mr. Lonely Heart," Denver says that he would never have thought that life could be so sweet.

"I believe that for all of us, one of the purposes of life, one of the processes of life is to find, to create, to determine and to define our own space. It's always there—it's never not there, but it takes time to see it or to feel it or to be able to communicate about it," he says.[6] In "Thanks to You," Denver sings that life has meaning.

In "Love Is Everywhere," Denver says that life is the fruit of one's own creation. He drinks his from a silver fountain. In this song, he states that he believes that life is perfect. At the end he adds that he knows this to be true. ". . . I made a choice a long time ago to give myself completely to life, and to take advantage of every opportunity I can to do the work I have to do to make my contribution in this world," states Denver.[7]

He sings about how the crew of Calypso works in the service of life and the living.[8] "It's a song of celebration and speaks of a commitment to make a contribution to life and to the quality of life on this planet," states Denver.[9] Then, he adds, "I also feel that commitment, that kind of ideal and purpose is what I do with my music."[10] In a short four-line song,[11] Denver praises the goodness of life. He says the same in "The Foxfire Suite: Spring Is Alive." Simply put: Life is good.

In order to experience life's goodness, Denver says that people must surrender to life. In "Sweet Surrender," he sings about living without care,

---

5. Denver, *Anthology*, 150.
6. Ibid., 192.
7. Ibid., 281.
8. "Calypso."
9. Denver, *Anthology*, 191.
10. Ibid.
11. "Life Is So Good."

like the fish in the ocean or like the birds in the air. "I believe we are all on the same path. It takes many different forms, is found in many different places, but we're all on the same path," Denver says. "Joy, really, is in surrendering to what life has to offer."[12] He expresses this same idea in "Hold on Tightly." He says that people have to hold on tightly, yet let go lightly, in order to surrender to life.

Denver believes that the way to live life is by learning from others. In "Rocky Mountain Suite (Cold Nights in Canada)," he says that a reason he went to a meadow in Jasper, Alberta, was to learn about life and death from the people who live in the high country of the Canadian Rocky Mountains. In another context, but appropriate nevertheless, Denver says, "Being . . . in the mountains, living the way we do, . . . does enhance your life."[13] Aspen is a life to live, he sings in "Aspenglow."

A person may be raised in hard times, but still have a good life.[14] Sometimes, a person may be willing to give up life in order to live. Such is the case in "For You." Denver says that he would give his life for the person he loves because that person is a reason for living. The other person is worth the sacrifice of the rest of his life. A person is willing to make this sacrifice if he or she can say to the other person that he or she would like to share life with the other.[15]

When loves fails, or the game is over, Denver says that life will not be the same.[16] In "Children of the Universe," he adds that it is important to understand that living life is more than choosing sides. And in "Opposite Tables," he cautions against being consumed in individual positions.

Denver says that even when people feel that life is not worth living that they should remember that life is sweet. In "Sweet, Sweet Life," he sings about living the day without being brought down. "As depressed as I was and as heavy as everything felt to me (life was not worth living), my absolute prayerful and agonizing cry was to live," says Denver,[17] when writing "Sweet, Sweet Life."

Similar thoughts are expressed in "Sticky Summer Weather." He sings about almost making his life worth living, but the reason is hiding behind

12. Denver, *Anthology*, 151.

13. Ibid., 25.

14. "Alaska and Me."

15. "Follow Me."

16. "The Game Is Over."

17. Denver, *Anthology*, 44.

the clouds, like the sun on an overcast day. Likewise, "Take Me to Tomorrow" asks questions about the quality of life. Denver sings about being satisfied with life; he invites the listener to reflect on its realness, happiness, and wastefulness. Denver says that when he gets lost in the sadness and the screams of life and is deep in despair, he looks in the center and suddenly everything's clear.[18] Then, he can dance in the circle of the love and light.[19]

In "Amazon (Let This Be a Voice)," Denver's philosophical song, he focuses on the song of life. He sings about the bird that sings in a jungle; that one song represents all music, and all songs about life are gathered together in that one song.

Even though Denver can say that life is so incredible to him,[20] that he lives his life in celebration that he has a life to live,[21] and expresses the desire that he wants to live forever,[22] in "Two Shots," he states that he knows that life is worth living, but sometimes it is not fair.

Experiences

In order to live life as fully as possible, one must be open to all of life's experiences. "What I am doing," Denver says about his music, "is bringing you into my life and bringing you into my views, my experiences...."[23] This means that on the road of experience[24] a person is open to new opportunities for himself or herself as well as listening to those of others.

One must want to live, grow, see, know, share, and be.[25] In "I Want to Live," on the album with the same name, Denver identifies some of his experiences, such as seeing the breaching of a whale in the ocean, dolphins frolicking in the ocean's foam, and hearing the humpback whale's call. In "Poems, Prayers, and Promises," he stresses the importance of reflecting on the experiences of life. He states that after thinking about all the things he has done and how his life has been, he names more experiences, such as seeing the sunshine, sleeping in the rain, spending several nights in the

18. "Looking for Space."
19. "Love Is Everywhere."
20. "Like a Sad Song."
21. "Anthem-Revelation."
22. "Zachary and Jennifer."
23. Denver, *Anthology*, 128.
24. "Looking for Space."
25. "I Want to Live."

wilderness alone, knowing sexual pleasures, having friends, and living in his home. He concludes by singing about how good it all is to be alive. Denver says that it is important to name the experiences of one's life as soon as possible because the days pass quickly or the nights are seldom long. He adds that it is important to remember that there's still so much to do, so many things his mind has never known. These same sentiments are echoed by Denver in "Season Suite: Summer." He calls life's experiences a tapestry and sings about many things that he has yet to see. Later in the song, he adds his understanding that the experiences of life help one see how all things and people are connected. He feels a part of everything he sees, and a part of everything he sees is in him.

In his songs, Denver likes to share his experiences with others. In "Annie's Song," the listener gets to peek in on a night in a forest, the mountains in springtime, a walk in the rain, a storm on the desert, and a sleepy blue ocean. In "Trade Winds," Denver mentions thunder, seas, and Rocky Mountain memories. And in "Rocky Mountain High," the listener participates with the twenty-seven-year-old man as he climbs cathedral mountains, sees silver clouds below, and gazes upon a clear, blue mountain lake. These experiences lead to a life that is full of wonder, but a heart that still knows some fear.

In "Children of the Universe," Denver explains that different people experience life in various ways. He sings about those who sail and fly and about those who seldom leave home.

The same idea is expressed in "Hold on Tightly." In that song he sings about what people value, such as fame over fortune and love over gold. Some people want power; some people never want to age. Other people live into the future, while some live in the past. There are people who have to be first, and there are those who are last. Even if a person thinks that his or her life is just a circus,[26] a circle of experiences in which there's nothing to learn of what life is all about, by listening to all the crazy things[27] another has seen, one can share the joys and sorrows of living. Denver makes this point in "Flying for Me," a song about NASA's Challenger. He says that he wanted to fly in a rocket. But, realizing that he couldn't join the crew, he knows that he could share in their experience. They were flying for him, he says. He adds that they gave their light, their spirit, and all they could be.

26. "Circus."
27. "Hitchhiker."

Changes

The lifetime journey of experiences which begins at birth, the questions one entertains and the answers for which one searches, and the hardy living that one engages in lead to changes. Denver asks about recognizing changes in nature in "Season Suite: Spring." He asks his listeners if they care about what is going on around them. He also asks if they can sense the changes coming to them. Referring to the effect of global warming, in "It's About Time," Denver says that it is time to recognize global warming. By recognizing the changes in nature, Denver believes that people can recognize that everything is about change.[28] In "Starwood in Aspen," he sings about seeing the shadows of changes, and in his ballad, "Rocky Mountain High," once the twenty-seven-year-old man discovers that life is nothing other than a series of alterations, he keeps changing fast. Denver's hope is that people will recognize, as he does, that worry about worldly ways and means are just changes as humankind moves on.[29]

Denver says that sometime changes frighten him, [30] but he also knows that all it takes is one man to change the world. In "What One Man Can Do," he sings about dreaming, loving, and changing the world to make it young again. In the same song, he says that one man can make the world new again and make it work again.

Denver believes that there comes a time when changes must be made. In "Circus," he sings about making mistakes again, changing the show, and finding another way. One change which must be made, says Denver, is the sale of weapons. He explains that he cannot take the guns anymore in "Sail Away Home." He also says that he cannot take the screams or the pain which result from so many guns being on the streets. He declares that it must stop; it must change. Such gun violence cannot continue.

Another change which must be made is found in "I Want to Live." In this song, Denver says hunger must be wiped out. Killing must stop. A respect for human life, sings Denver, is an idea whose time has come.

Denver believes in change. Humankind can find a better way he says in "Rhymes and Reasons." In "The Eagle and the Hawk," he calls upon all people to hope for the future. He says that change will enable all people to be all they can and not what they are.

---

28. "Love Is the Master."
29. "To the Wild Country."
30. "Poems, Prayers, and Promises."

Self-Discovery

The idea of being all that it is possible for people to be stems from Denver's on-going journey of self-discovery. Sometimes he refers to this process as simply growing up, as in "Alaska and Me." In this song he sings about growing up and going to school. He also explains how hard it is to get into life on one's own; sometimes it looks like a person is losing, but he or she can turn the struggles into winning. Similarly, growing up is the idea found in "Wild Montana Skies." Denver sings about an orphan who grows up as a farmer. The ballad speaks about the young man leaving home the day before he turned twenty-one. It is not until much later in his life that he finds himself. Denver says that when the young man turned thirty, he stopped running and found his way home.

Denver's most complete treatment of growing up as self-discovery is found in "Come and Let Me Look in Your Eyes." He begins the song by saying that physical growing is not hard to do; it can be measured by marks on the wall or door frame. A person, who was once two feet high, may grow into one who is six feet tall. But there is more than just physical growing, as Denver explains in the next stanza of the song. A person must learn to listen to the advice of others; without listening words are like seasons of the wind. In the refrain, he says that real growth occurs when a person finds himself or herself. The third and fourth stanzas of this song explain that self-discovery is not found in rules, listening, reading, or just doing what is right. Some who think that is the way to self-discovery often end up lost. After further reflection, found in the last stanza, Denver says that real self-discovery is facing oneself; when one does that, there is no place to hide.

In "Looking for Space," Denver brings together his themes of journey and self-discovery. On the road of experience, he sings, a person tries to find his or her own way. Sometimes one is moving, and sometimes one is standing still. The refrain of this song even more explicitly communicates the search for self. Denver sings about his search for space to find out who he is so that he can know and understand himself. When Denver wrote this song, he says, "I was looking to find out what my space is, what the area is that I occupy, and what space my ideas, my intentions, and my purposes are . . . ."[31] The themes of journey and self-discovery are also intertwined in "Love Is the Master." Denver says that he has been on a journey of self-discovery which may lead him home.

31. Denver, *Anthology*, 192.

Denver also believes that self-discovery can take place by paying attention to the changes in the seasons of the year. In "Season Suite: Spring," he asks the listener if he or she can see himself or herself reflected in the seasons, and if he or she can understand the need to continue on.

In a number of his songs Denver exhorts people to be all that they can be and all that they ever longed for, as in "The Gold and Beyond." He sings about the spirit burning inside a person to be the best in the world. That fire sparks one to go faster and further than anyone else. That flame engenders bravery and strength. Likewise, in "Love Is Everywhere," Denver says that a person who becomes all he or she can be must pursue self-discovery even more.

When a person no longer knows himself or herself, then the time to rediscover one's self has arrived. Denver muses on this in "Some Days Are Diamonds (Some Days Are Stone)." He compares losing self-knowledge to seeing himself as a stranger in the mirror. His reflection reminds him that he has become what he never thought he would be. A similar idea is expressed in "Circus." Denver sings about having lost what he was searching for and having nothing left to share. Such a realization spurs him to take time for self by going somewhere else. Failing to do so results in a frenzied pursuit of looking for himself but not finding himself.

In "To the Wild Country," Denver expresses the fear of losing self. He begins this song by singing about his fear of losing himself and not knowing who he is. After getting caught up in life's struggles, he feels as if his back is against a stone wall or like his finger is in the dam keeping it from bursting. He's gradually losing strength and falling down. Then, he says that by turning his heart to wild Alaska he is able to find himself again, an idea he also expresses at the end of "Trade Winds." In this song, thunder and ocean—along with memories of the Rocky Mountains—help him find himself.

Growing Old

The journey of a lifetime involves not only self-discovery and being all that one can be, but it also entails growing old. Denver says that he can get excited about growing old. In fact, in "Poems, Prayer, and Promises," he says that when he thinks of growing old, he is turned on! In "Hold on Tightly," he says that some people never want to grow old. In "All of My Memories," he says that he is looking for somewhere to grow old.

"Whispering Jessie" is a song about Jessie, who lives in Denver's heart. In one stanza of the song he sings about the limitations of getting old. In this song the limitation is being a cowboy from the Colorado high country who is too old to ride his horse.

Dreams

Growing old is only part of the bigger picture of life for Denver. He sings about the importance of dreaming of the future, of having a vision, and of wishing for a better world. In "Children of the Universe," he sings about a heritage of vision that most people share. And in "Around and Around," he sings about dreams that are full of promises and hopes for the future. In "Higher Ground," he sings about the dream he has and how he must live up to it. His dream enables him to reach for the higher ground. He emphasizes this even more when he sings about standing on his own and living his vision.

Denver says that people should hope for the future.[32] In "Rhymes and Reasons," he concretizes this hope in children, who serve as a promise for the future. So, he invites the listener to come and join him in order to find a better way. It is Denver's belief that all rise with the same vision, or all fall without it.

In "Take Me to Tomorrow," Denver asks questions in order to stress the importance of dreaming. He asks the listener about his or her dreams, plans, and schemes. In "Poems, Prayers, and Promises," Denver says it is good to ask about dreams. "I have a vision of tomorrow out there working, a world that works, and that's where I want to be," says Denver.[33]

He acknowledges that sometimes dreams go dry,[34] and he says that people have dreams they cannot remember, hopes they have forgotten, and memories that have faded. However, he adds that when a dream is lost,[35] or when it becomes a road to nowhere,[36] all one can do is dream again.[37] This does not mean dreaming away, as in escaping from reality, but it implies

32. "The Eagle and the Hawk."
33. Denver, *Anthology*, 25.
34. "Fly Away."
35. "It's a Possibility."
36. "To the Wild Country."
37. "What One Man Can Do."

looking into the mind and making plans to see things one needs to see, but, even more importantly, thinking about who one wants to be.[38]

Denver says that there is a dimension of love that involves dreaming. In "A Wild Heart Looking for Home," he says that he is dreaming of touching the face of his lover in the moonlight. He explains that dreaming cannot fit in a cage. In the final stanza of this song, he expresses the depth of his love for his beloved by thinking of her face, a vision he has and holds.

In "Dreamland Express," he tells the one he loves that he could not believe that his dream would come true. Later, he asks this person to let him be the one that she dreams of. Then, he goes so far as to say that he gets a vision of heaven with her with him.

He's a man without a dream in "Thanks to You." But then a person he loves comes along, and he knows where he's going and what he wants to do. He sings about looking into the other's eyes and dreaming about her forever. Similarly, in "The Gift You Are," he tells his beloved that she is a gift to him because she enables all his dreams to come true. Then, he adds that she is the promise of all the ages; she is the vision of prophets and sages.

Denver equates prophecy with dreaming of the future, as can be seen in the line above from "The Gift You Are." In "Dancing with the Mountains," a song about the unity of people and the earth engaged in a cosmic dance, Denver sings about hearing the prophet tell his tale. Likewise, in "Stonehaven Sunset," Denver sings about the destruction of the earth, saying that the ecological prophets laugh because they foretold global warming.

The last stanza of "The Gift You Are" is addressed to the listener. In it Denver encourages dreaming. He sings about dreaming of a brighter tomorrow and trusting that the dream will come true. Then, he says that the dream should be captured in a crystal jar so that the person can become aware of what a gift she is.

Denver dreams about a variety of things in his songs. He dreams of Alaska so far away in "Alaska and Me." In the same song he says that he dreams of flying over mountains and glaciers. In "Falling Leaves (The Refugees)," after comparing refugees to the leaves that fall from the trees, he expresses his dream for a new spring that blesses the falling leaves. "Looking for Space," Denver's song about self-discovery, also contains a refrain about dreaming. Denver says that self-discovery is a sweet dream. He adds that there are times when the dream looks achievable, and there are times when it looks like it is not.

38. "Sail Away Home."

The transcendental dimension of dreaming, which is found in the fly-ing like an eagle metaphor in "Looking for Space," is also found in "Eagles and Horses (I'm Flying Again)." In the refrain of this song Denver sings about his vision of eagles and horses. The horses are on a ridge, racing the wind. The eagles go higher and higher, while the horses run faster and fast-er. To understand this song's refrain, the listener is told that eagles represent the soul, and horses represent the body. Thus, while the body is tied to the earth, the soul soars to the heavens in dreams.

In "On the Wings of a Dream," Denver also expresses this transcen-dental dimension of dreaming. He begins the song by singing about a dream of dying, being laid to rest, and then flying. The cosmic dimension of dreaming is expressed in "It's About Time." Denver writes that it is time to turn around the world by making it the dream people know it can be.

Denver employs the metaphor of islands for dreams in "Islands." He says that he dreams of home, and the islands are like so many dreams. He adds that in dreams no one is really present because the dreamer is always alone. As the subject of "The Gold and Beyond," dreaming is pictured as a person's goal. Denver sings about how in a moment a dream of a lifetime can be won.

No matter what the type of dream, Denver considers it important that all people have a vision of the future, which should include heaven. He ex-presses this best in his philosophical song, "Amazon (Let This Be a Voice)." He sings about a vision that shines brightly in the darkness. That one vision represents all the dreams of people everywhere, and all of the dreams of everyone are contained in that one. Later in the song, he says that this is a vision of heaven. Then, he petitions the listener to let his song be one for dreamers.

Falling into Love

Life involves love—falling into it and falling out of it—for Denver. In "Love Is Everywhere," he says that he can see it, and in "Heart to Heart," he says that he can know safely and truly that love is everywhere.

Love is just a way to live and die, Denver sings in "Matthew." In "It Makes Me Giggle," he refers to love as sweet as candy. In his attempt to describe love in his many love songs, Denver uses a variety of metaphors, which are summarized in "For You." This song serves as an outline for a presentation of his images of love. He sings about looking into his lover's eyes, laying in her arms, being there for her, living in her laughter, singing in her heart, being her dreams come true, sitting by her window, touching her during the night, praying each day for her, longing for her kisses, dreaming by her side, and giving his life for her. Later in the song he adds that love is waking up each morning in the presence of his beloved, having her at his side, knowing that she is never far away, being his reason for life, adoring her, and knowing that she is in his heart. Then, he adds that love is a love song, the beat of the heart, and the pledge of life.

Denver says that love is looking into the eyes of the loved one. In "Thanks to You," he says that he looks into her eyes and dream about her. In "For Baby (For Bobbie)," he says that the happiness he has found is a reflection of the love in her eyes. He asks his beloved if her tears belong to him in "My Sweet Lady." Likewise, in "Goodbye Again," as he prepares to leave, he says that she turns away and begins to cry because he is leaving. In "My Sweet Lady," Denver calms her when he tells her to close her eyes; he promises to remain at her side.

Love is lying in the arms of the beloved. Denver indicates this in "Thanks to You" when he says that lying in the arms of his beloved gives him great pleasure. In "Goodbye Again," he regrets having to leave his soft and warm lover, so he decides to lie down again and hold her in his arms. Likewise, in "Whispering Jessie," he says that he longs to hold her. He expresses regret in "The Game Is Over," when he says that life is not the same without his lover because he cannot hold her in his arms. And in "Annie's Song," he refers to lying in the arms of his lover as dying, when he petitions her to let him die in her arms.

A theme similar to lying in the arms of one's lover is expressed as lying by the side of the beloved. Lying by his beloved's side is the greatest peace he has ever known, sings Denver in "Goodbye Again." In "Annie's Song," he turns this into a petition, requesting that he lay down beside her. In "My Sweet Lady," he addresses his beloved lady and tells her that he is as close as he can be. Then he swears that their time together has just begun. He just wants to lay his tired old body down in "Back Home Again," presumably near the one he loves. In "Shanghai Breezes," he paints a picture of two lovers in the night, unafraid in the dark. Similarly, in "Thanks to You," he sings about lovers who have spent the night together, wake up together, and plan their day together. According to Denver, that is what gives meaning to life.

Lying in the arms of one's lover and lying by the side of one's lover means that there is some touching involved. Denver sings about the way his beloved likes to touch him in "Somethin' About." In "Hey There, Mr. Lonely Heart," he wants to know the answer to the mystery of love's most precious seed, asking if it is found in a touch. He expresses his desire to experience the touch of Jessie's cool hands on his fevered brow in "Whispering Jessie," while in "Back Home Again," he says that he wants to feel his lover's fingers feather-soft upon him. In order for true love to occur, Denver says that his heart must be open and tender to the touch in "True Love Takes Time." Touching can heal, as Denver expresses in "True Love Takes Time." He sings about the love that heals through one's hands.

For some people love is a way to feel, says Denver in "Perhaps Love." In "Back Home Again," he says that his old farm feels like a long-lost friend. In "Daydream," he tells his lover that he writes songs just to try and tell her how he really feels.

Only in "Whispering Jessie" does Denver employ the auditory sense when he tells his lover he longs to hear her soft breathing.

While either lying in his lover's arms or lying beside her, Denver says that he dreams of his beloved. He expresses this in "My Sweet Lady." In "Daydream," he says that he remembers dreaming with his beloved.

Even if the lover is far away, there is still a feeling of closeness. The first verse of "Shanghai Breezes" says that talking on the telephone makes him feel as if his lover is next door when in fact she is a world away. Later in the song, Denver says that he feels close to her, even though they are separated by half a million miles. She is alive and living in his heart.

Love is also characterized as dreams that come true[39] by Denver. True love is the only dream he knows, he says in the last line of "Seasons of the Heart." In "Shanghai Breezes," he tells his lover that she is in his dreams and always near, and her face in his dreams is like heaven to him.

In "For You," Denver says that love is being there for the beloved. He wants to be the first one always there for her. In "For Baby (For Bobbie)," he expresses the same sentiment when he promises that he will be there for her when she is feeling down. In "Whispering Jessie," being there for the other means riding by Denver's side. Feeling is involved in "Shanghai Breezes." The soft and gentle breezes remind Denver of his beloved's tenderness.

39. "Perhaps Love."

Love involves laughter and kisses. He remembers laughing all the time when his lover belonged to him in "Daydream." In "Annie's Song," he asks her to let him drown in her laughter.

Country love is kisses in the kitchen, states Denver in "Country Love." In "Back Home Again," he says that he longs for the kisses, because there is something special about the way the lips of his lover meet his.[40] He wants to know if the answer to the mystery of precious love is found in a kiss in "Hey There, Mr. Lonely Heart." In "Goodbye Again," he tells his lover that he longs to kiss her tears away and give her back her smile. Similar sentiments are expressed in "For Baby (For Bobbie)" when he says that he will be there to kiss away her tears if she cries.

Love involves openness, like that of windows and doors. In "Heart to Heart," Denver sings about giving his heart to the person he loves as she gives hers to him. Likewise, in "Perhaps Love," Denver proposes that love is like a window or an open door that invites one to come closer in order to disclose more. In this same song, Denver employs a variety of metaphors for love. In the first verse he proposes that love is like a place to rest, to find shelter from a storm, and to keep warm. In the third verse he says that love is like a cloud and as strong as steel. For others love is a way of life or a way one feels. Denver proposes that love is like the ocean constantly changing and like a warming fire when it is cold. He also compares it to thunder during rain. Echoing the last line of this song, in "True Love Takes Time," Denver says that he gives all his rainy days to the person he loves.

Love involves spending time with the lover. True love takes time, he sings over and over again in "True Love Takes Time." The sweetest thing Denver knows is spending time with his lover, he says in "Back Home Again." In "My Sweet Lady," he asks his lover if she thinks their time together is all gone. He answers his question by swearing that their time has just begun. Later in this song he characterizes spending time with the other as entwining. He says that the day their lives were joined that they became entwined. This leads him to request that she let him always be with her in "Annie's Song." After lamenting the fact that he has to leave his beloved in "Goodbye Again," he states that the time they have is worth the time alone.

Spending time with the person one loves involves walking together and holding hands. In "Shanghai Breezes," Denver sings about walking hand-in-hand in a park with his beloved and seeing other lovers who walk alone. Denver remembers walking with his lover in "Daydream," and

40. "Somethin' About."

clinging to the warmth of her hand in "For Baby (For Bobbie)." Denver begins the second verse of "Seasons of the Heart" by singing about walking beside his beloved in the evening chill. And in "Country Love," Denver characterizes country love as silky nights and warm familiar hands.

Denver compares love to light. He expresses his love in "Somethin' About," saying that it makes his light shine. Similarly, in "Heart to Heart," he says that love is a light that shines from one heart to another. In "Back Home Again," Denver says that love lights his way, and the light in his beloved's eyes makes him warm. Denver says his response is to give all his sunshine to the one he loves.

The light of love brings happiness. In "My Sweet Lady," he asks his lover if she is happy. He expresses this feeling in "Back Home Again" by singing about the happiness that living with his beloved brings him. In "For Baby (For Bobbie)," he promises to share all the happiness he has found with his beloved.

According to Denver, those who are in love must understand what it is all about. He says it may involve talking without speaking, that is, looking at the beloved and knowing all there is to know.[41] He emphasizes talking again in "Daydream," remembering talking to his lover. And in "True Love Takes Time," he says that he will give his beloved all the time it takes to understand. Being more direct in "Follow Me," Denver says that he will try to find the way that he can make his lover understand.

Sometimes what needs to be understood are love's meanings that his beloved has never seen before.[42] In "For Baby (For Bobbie)," he promises to do anything to help her understand while loving her more than anyone else can. He also emphasizes the need for understanding in "Country Love." He says that country love consists of understanding, honesty, and truthfulness.

For understanding to take place between two lovers, they must be willing to talk to each other, or as Denver says in "Two Shots" find someone who's willing to share and have something in common. Denver reminiscences about this in "The Game Is Over" when he says that he remembers the things shared when hearts were beating together. In "Seasons of the Heart," he specifically states that he and his beloved held much in common and shared many things. In "Hey There, Mr. Lonely Heart," Denver asks if the answer to the mystery of love's most precious seed is that it is really love itself that always wants to give. After further reflection he thinks that life

41. "The Game Is Over."
42. "My Sweet Lady."

would be sweet and love would be strong if people would gather and share with each other because the universal aspect of love is everywhere; what differs is only the name given to love. Later in the song, Denver restates the idea that a reason to love is because within the heart true love is all that is needed. Denver then advocates that people live by giving the gift of love.

Denver believes that one person has to call another to love. In "Annie's Song," he petitions her to let him love her, to let him give his life to her. Later, he petitions her to let him love her, to let him love her again. He echoes this sentiment in "Dreamland Express" when he requests that his lover let him be the one that she loves. The other person gives a name to love, or, as Denver expresses in "Thanks to You," love has a name.

Love is physically located in a person's heart. The heart is a hunter sings Denver in "Its' a Possibility." In "Whispering Jessie," Denver says that his love for Jessie lives in his heart. Similarly, in "Shanghai Breezes," he sings to his beloved, telling her that she is in his heart and living there. When the love of another lives in one's heart, physical presence is not always needed. Denver states this in a question in "Goodbye Again." He asks his lover if she thinks that if he were always present their love would be the same. He answers this by saying that being physically apart is important in a love relationship. People need time alone as well as together.

According to Denver, love is like a song that he remembers singing.[43] Sometimes, the lyrics are sad, and at other times they are happy, sings Denver in "Country Love." He sings a beautiful love song in "Thanks to You." He calls his beloved his lucky star that came like a special song to his lonely heart. In "For Baby (For Bobbie)," he promises his lover that he will sing her a song of the rainbow that whispers his joy. Denver says that sometimes he cannot find the words that express what he wants to say,[44] but the struggle bears fruit, as later he sings that his beloved is in his dreams and always near him, especially when he sings his songs. He discovers that she is living in his heart. In "True Love Takes Time," he declares that he has been looking for someone to sing harmony with him. Together, he and his lover would become a love song.

A similar idea is found in "Hey There, Mr. Lonely Heart." The title of the song indicates that someone has a lonely heart. Denver says that if one has a lonely heart, this song is just for him or her. In the heart of all, true love is all a person needs.

43. "Daydream."
44. "Shanghai Breezes."

In "Perhaps Love," Denver contrasts two different perspectives of love. He sings about those who say that love is holding on and those who say that love is letting go. Likewise, in "Seasons of the Heart," he phrases it as growing together or drifting apart. He also expresses the paradox of love as coming and going. The holding-on theme is emphasized in "Opposites Tables" when Denver asks if there is a vision of love that binds people together.

The letting-go theme is found in "I'd Rather Be a Cowboy." In this song about Jessie's departure, Denver sings that after all the time spent together, it is hard to see her go, but, he says, he loves her just enough to let her go. Also, in "Goodbye Again," the letting-go aspect of love permeates the whole song, especially the refrain in which Denver expresses his sorrow to be leaving his lover. Both his lover's tears and their fight before his departure make it difficult for Denver to leave, to let go.

Besides promising his beloved that he will do anything to keep her satisfied,[45] Denver says that the greatest love is his willingness to give up his life for his lover. He expresses this in "Annie's Song" when he asks her to let him love her, to let him give his life to her. In "For You," he expressly states he gives his life for her. It is the chorus of this song, however, which demonstrates his supreme sacrifice. He sings about his love being for the rest of his life.

It is not difficult to see the reflection of Jesus' words in John's Gospel in Denver's song. The Johannine Jesus says, "No one has greater love than this, to lay down one's life for one's friends" (John 15:13). There is also an echo of another passage in John's Gospel in which Jesus says: "I give you a new commandment: love one another. As I have loved you, so you also should love one another. This is how all will know that you are my disciples, if you have love for one another" (John 13:34–35).

Denver's various metaphors for falling into love can best be summarized in two lines of "Perhaps Love." He sings that some people say that love is everything, and some people say that they do not know. The bottom line, according to Denver, is all a man can do is love.[46]

Falling out of Love

Denver's metaphors for falling out of love are not as numerous as those he uses for falling into love. Even though he says that he does not believe true

45. "For Baby (For Bobbie)."
46. "What One Man Can Do."

love ever ends,[47] he speaks about broken hearts, broken lives, and families that love has split apart in "Country Love." Collectively, he refers to all of this as love gone wrong.

Just as "For You" serves as a guide through Denver's metaphors for falling into true love, so "Falling out of Love" serves as an outline of his images for falling out of love. In the chorus he sings that falling out of true love is like losing one's best friend. In the first verse he sings about not having anyone to talk with or listen to, and words don't matter anyway because they cannot describe the pain or the fear. In the second verse he describes how there is no hope for a future. The nights grow cold and hard to live through, yet one hates to see the mornings come. The next day matters little because there is little future and life seems to be finished. The third verse tries to articulate the sentiments felt in the heart when one has fallen out of love. The heart does not flutter. There are no lover's eyes to see. The world seems to fall down around one. Denver communicates a sense of failure in the last verse, expressing love and dreams lost.

In "In My Heart," he also describes falling out of love as losing his best friend. At the beginning of this song, he indicates that people can live together but really be far apart for most of the time. In "Seasons of the Heart," he describes this as discovering a stranger in one's own home. Even while lying right beside the beloved, one can feel alone. In "In My Heart," he says that he doesn't want to talk about this experience of falling out of love. He sings about ringing in his ears and looking to the ocean to wash him away. While he might be willing to speak about his experience of falling out of love in "Seasons of the Heart," he says that he doesn't know how to tell this part of his story because he never imagined it would happen this way.

It is the pain of falling out of love that Denver focuses on in "The Game Is Over." To his beloved he says that life will not be the same without her to ease the pain and remember when their love was a reason for living. Likewise, in "Thought of You," he says that the memories of love a year ago still bring tears to his eyes. Then, he explains that the pain is caused by the thought of his beloved. In "A Country Girl in Paris," the pain is described as a broken heart. First, Denver says, the country girl's heart is filled with pain. Then, he sings about life being hard, that is, being alone in Paris while one's lover is far away. Later in the song, Denver speaks about the broken heart as the loss of innocence that is linked with the pain. He sings about once one's heart is open to another's love nothing can be the same again. In "Seasons

47. "Falling out of Love."

of the Heart," Denver also describes a broken heart. He characterizes it as emptiness inside and as a longing for things that have been denied.

The solution to a broken heart is found in "A Country Girl in Paris." Denver says that the way to heal a broken heart is to give love just one more chance. This way to heal a broken heart is also given voice in "Never a Doubt." In this song Denver says that a broken heart is tragic, but it can be mended again. In "Love Again," a song about falling in love a second time, Denver also sings about the pain of love. He wonders if he has given up on romance and wonders if he can love again. He describes how a person in pain attempts to close himself off from the rest of the world; he compares it to closing windows and locking doors. Yet, even then he wants more. Finally, he recognizes that hiding is a contradiction when it comes to love. He says that he was afraid that he might never love again.

In "In My Heart," Denver says that falling out of love makes him feel like life is an illusion. He explains this feeling in the chorus of "I Can't Escape." He says that he cannot escape thinking about the person he loves every day, wishing that she were his or caring for her. In this song he also says that music on the radio reminds him of his broken heart. Other things also remind him of his broken heart, such as a morning rain, a cold night, and an inside ache.

Probably Denver's most simple statement of this feeling is found in "Like a Sad Song." He sings about feeling like a sad song, feeling all alone without his beloved. This feeling of being sad and trapped in his memories also pervades "Thought of You." In this song Denver sings about not finding a way to erase how he feels. He remembers the passion of the relationship. This same feeling of being trapped in a broken heart with one's memories pervades "I Remember Romance." Denver sings about remembering romance, bubble baths, breakfast, and love by candlelight. He also says he remembers lying in his beloved's arms, her hair across his shoulder, her breast upon his arm, and laughing at the moon, dancing at the rainbow's end, and losing her too soon. He concludes this song by expressing forgiveness.

While Denver acknowledges the differences between two lovers, as he does in "Seasons of the Heart" when he sings about differences being as natural as the changing of the seasons, he also knows that when people are going in different directions, true love will have to wait, as he explains in "Two Different Directions." The song emphasizes the opposite ends of the spectrum of two people. Denver says that two people come from different places with different points of view and find themselves in different spaces with everything being new. One person is always on the road somewhere while the other one always stays home. One person always wants to work things out while the other one wants to play. Denver further characterizes these two people as one being like an open window and one just like a closing door, and one liking to see the morning sunrise while the other one sleeps in late.

What causes love to fail? In "Two Different Directions," Denver says that old patterns of behavior rise to the surface, and those cause anger, insensitive spoken words, and broken hearts. Neither person expresses his or her deepest feelings. Such pretending leads to different directions.

Even after falling out of love, Denver presents his need to have feminine companionship in a rag-time type song entitled "Deal with the Ladies." He sings about making them sigh and cry over him. Throughout the song, he expresses his desire to swing with the good times and to have ladies around wondering where he's been. He says that he likes to make it tough for them never to get enough of him.

Loneliness

Closely allied to, and an effect of, a broken heart is loneliness. Denver sings about being alone, empty, and lonely. In "True Love Takes Time," Denver says that he has been alone for many years. He emphasizes this more in "Love Again" when he sings about being convinced that he would be lonely for the rest of his life. And Denver gives clearest expression of his concept of loneliness in "Never a Doubt." He sings that he never doubted that people were meant to be lonely! He explains that this feeling is like being in a room filled with darkness without a window. He says to the listener that there must have been moments when he or she felt truly alone.

The mind runs wild when one is all alone, sings Denver in "Whispering Jessie." This can lead to a feeling of being all alone in the world, as he sings in "Looking for Space." When a person feels all alone in the universe, he or she is lost in sadness.

One of Denver's favorite descriptions of loneliness is facing a sleepless night all alone.[48] In his whole song dedicated to this topic, "Sleepin' Alone," he says that a person can be a millionaire and still be sleeping alone. He sings about one night stands being better than sleeping alone and

---

48. "I Can't Escape."

how having someone present who doesn't really care is worse than sleeping alone. One effect of sleeping alone is drinking alcohol, states Denver. And another is praying to God that the night will end quickly. The chorus of "Prisoners (Hard Life, Hard Times)" also emphasizes the difficulty of spending a night all alone.

After saying that he has been thinking about his beloved all night long in "Daydream," Denver sings about not facing the night alone. Likewise, after saying that all his lover's nights have gone sad and shady in "Fly Away," he sings that in the world there's nobody as lonely as she. He adds a feeling of being lost in the midst of loneliness by singing about nowhere to go.

In "All of My Memories," Denver characterizes loneliness as spending nights in old motels sleeping alone. Later in the song, after lamenting his life in the city and the fact that a street taxi dancer was trying to save him from being alone, he says that experience was much worse than lonely when there is no place he really belongs.

Similar sentiments are expressed in "A Wild Heart Looking for Home." He sings about almost getting caught being lost alone in the night with nowhere to hide while crying inside. Later, he adds an expression of how loneliness makes him feel. He says that living without his lover makes the days endless. In "I'd Rather Be a Cowboy," he characterizes this sentiment as missing the person whom he had loved in the morning when he awoke alone. He adds that the absence of her laughter is a cold and empty sound.

There was never a doubt, sings Denver in "Never a Doubt," that after nights alone followed by desperate mornings that people were meant to be lonely. However, he does seem to move toward a moment of happiness later in the song, as he sings about sad nights turning into light-filled mornings with the hope that one's true love will come.

Besides imaging loneliness as spending the night all alone, Denver also pictures it as days on the road with no one beside him in "All of My Memories." Likewise, in "Annie's Other Song," he sings about being out on the road alone. It becomes a long lonesome ride in "Rocky Mountain Suite (Cold Nights in Canada)" and a lonesome old doggie in "Song of Wyoming."

Denver says that it is during times of trouble when one feels most alone in "Perhaps Love." In "Some Days Are Diamonds (Some Days Are Stone)," he says that sometimes the hard times won't leave him alone. He can't escape the difficulties in his life.

Denver says that he can't remember when he has ever been so lonely in "Starwood in Aspen," a song about being away from his home and family.

After losing the person he loves, he expresses a sentiment similar to that in "Starwood in Aspen" when he sings that he never felt so much alone.[49] Such experience of loneliness leads one to forget his or her purpose and even to lose faith. In "In My Heart," Denver asks four questions about loneliness, sadness, purpose, and faith.

Denver says that there are a number of signs of loneliness. In "Country Love," he states that Nashville tears are lonely signs that point to broken hearts, and that lonely words speak of love gone wrong. Nashville nights are lonely roads that all have traveled. The contrast in this song is between healthy love in the country and lonely love in the city.

In "A Wild Heart Looking for a Home," Denver pushes to an extreme the idea of being alone in the city as a sign of loneliness. He sings about life in the city getting all closed in to the point that a person can be in a crowd all alone and wishing that someone might phone. In "Falling Leaves (The Refugees)," he continues this theme, singing about refugees who are on a city street alone.

Loneliness is caused by the absence of one's lover. In "I'm Sorry," after thinking about how bad it feels being alone again, Denver says that he is sorry that things are not what they used to be. Then, he adds that more than anything else he is sorry for himself because his beloved is not with him. Later in the song, he adds that he is sorry for himself because his lover went away and sorry for himself for living without the one he loves. In "Like a Sad Song," he expresses it as feeling like a sad song, being all alone without his beloved.

In "Leaving on a Jet Plane," even before he leaves the person he loves, he says that he is already so lonesome that he could die. He urges his beloved to dream about the future when he will not have to leave alone. Similarly, in "Circus," he says that he informs his lover when he's lonely, but she does not think that he will leave, even though he must. But in "Follow Me," he says that he wants, nevertheless, to share his life with the person he loves. He would like to have her beside him and never be alone.

However, this same song also introduces another of Denver's expressions of loneliness—that of being with one's lover but still feeling alone. In "Follow Me," he says that the hardest thing he has ever done is to be so in love with his beloved and yet so alone. The same idea is expressed in "Seasons of the Heart." In this song Denver sings about how his lover has

---

49. "Singing Skies and Dancing Waters."

become a stranger in their home and how even lying beside her makes him feel alone.

In "Heart to Heart," Denver says that the other side of lonely is falling in love again. He expresses this same idea in "Thanks to You." To the person who came into his life Denver sings that she is like a special song to his lonely heart.

Understanding the effect that loneliness has on a person, in "Trade Winds" Denver promises his beloved that he will never leave her on the edge all alone. Such a positive attitude toward being alone also permeates "Islands." In this song Denver sings about never feeling alone when he is on the islands or in the highlands. However, he quickly lapses back into his usual expression of loneliness. The islands are like canyons with no one there, and the dreamer is always alone.

A positive attitude about being alone is expressed best in Denver's "Goodbye Again." He seems to be saying that being alone is as important as being together for a love relationship to flourish. Also, the time he and his beloved spend apart is a necessary prelude to the time they are able to spend together.

Denver says that everyone is afraid of being alone. In "The Harder They Fall," he devotes the last stanza to this topic; he emphasizes that no one wants to be alone and the fear of being alone. In "Downhill Stuff," he sings about looking for heaven and hope, but no one wants to look for those alone.

Service

Life for John Denver involves serving others in some manner. Life is not oriented just to self-pleasure. It is centered on giving and receiving. In "Aspenglow," Denver sings about his life in Aspen, Colorado, where there are ample opportunities to give. He also touches on another truth, namely, that a person receives much when he or she gives.

Denver demonstrated his own sense of service as the founder of The Windstar Foundation, which supported the Windstar Project, "a research and education center devoted to developing workable models for scientific and technological progress which retain a sense of harmony among people working together, between mankind and the physical environment, and between our everyday concerns and our own spirituality."[50] The Windstar

50. Denver, *Anthology*, 7.

Foundation lasted until October 2012—fifteen years after Denver's death—when its board of directors decided to dissolve it; the property was sold in 2013.

In "Calypso," Denver praises the crew of Calypso for working in the service of life and the living. Likewise, he begins "It Amazes Me" with the idea of one man seeking a way to help others. The man seeks truth and understanding while looking for answers to his questions. He wants to serve his brothers and sisters by sharing what was given to him.

Service takes the form of a teacher-student relationship in "Rocky Mountain Suite (Cold Nights in Canada)." Of the two men who are camped in a meadow in Jasper, Alberta, Denver says that one serves as a teacher while the other is the beginner who wants to learn. In "Matthew," service takes the form of easing another's burden on a farm. Denver says that his Uncle Matthew came to live with him in order to help his father work the land.

Joy

Being of service brings joy. In "Farewell Andromeda (Welcome to My Morning)," Denver sings about his welcome of others to share his happiness. He welcomes the listener to his happiness. While he smiles, he wants the listener to know that he is pleased to have him or her there, where, hopefully, he or she will welcome others and begin a meaningful conversation.

Denver expresses the joy of life in "Matthew" when he says that joy was just a thing that his uncle was raised on. Later in the song he expresses the same idea again while recounting how his uncle grew up in Kansas as a farm boy, who sat on his father's shoulders while his dad walked behind the mule pulling the plow on sunny days.

In "Aspenglow," joy is found in smiling faces all around when laughter is the only sound. Similarly, it was Denver's desire to hear the sound of lovely laughter in the air at Woodstock in "I Wish I Could Have Been There (Woodstock)." In "Annie's Song," his poetic request to his beloved is to drown in her laughter. And in "Zachary and Jennifer," he speaks of his son, Zachary, as shining laughter in the sun. In trying to describe how precious the gift that one person is to another in "The Gift You Are," Denver says that he or she is all the joy that love can bring.

Magic

In three songs Denver characterizes the joy that love can bring as magic. He doesn't mean the current understanding of magic as the ability to pull a rabbit out of a hat or the illusionist ability to make things disappear. In "The Music Is You," a four-line song, he sings about the magic of music to make pictures and tell stories. Commenting on this song, he explains what he means by magic: ". . . The music is out there. I just happen to be the guy listening when that particular song floated by that day. It's your music. I'm more a vehicle or a tool for putting it down, but it's your music. So, you know what music does for me, that it makes pictures, it tells stories. It's all there, but the music is you; the magic is you."[51] Some people might refer to Denver's magic as inspiration, the hidden promptings of the Spirit of God.

Denver captures the same idea found in "The Music Is You" in two questions in "Love Again." He wants to know what it takes for a blind man to see. He draws out a parallel between the blind man seeing and the magic that transforms a sigh into a song.

In "Never a Doubt," he spends time exploring the magic of love. He says that there are people who do not believe in magic. For them the magic of love does not exist. This makes their life nothing but pleasure or pain.

Thus, magic is that which people experience in loving and drinking deeply of the precious fountain of life, which gushes with love, loneliness, service, and joy.

Memories

For Denver, as a person makes his or her journey from birth to death, seeking answers to questions, living, changing, growing, dreaming, falling into love, and falling out of love, such a one collects many memories. Denver sings about memories. In "Matthew," he indicates that some of his memories came from his uncle. He sings about the stories his uncle told him and the experiences they shared together—Denver's memories. The verses of that song serve as an example of what Denver calls memories that can't grow old in "Aspenglow."

In "Poems, Prayers, and Promises," Denver understands that some memories are collective; they are shared by a number of people. Faded memories, such as those found in "Around and Around," are also a part of

---

51. Denver, *Anthology*, 151.

life. Nevertheless, Denver says that he loves to remember. And so in "Daydream," he makes a list of what he remembers doing with the person he loves. He remembers talking to her, and walking, laughing, singing, dreaming, and loving with her.

Even if the remembering is painful, the memories should not be lost. After realizing this, in "All of My Memories," Denver sings about his memories lying on the highway of life. Later in the song, while he says he is leaving all his memories behind in the city to seek out a better life in the country, he knows, nevertheless, that memories cannot be erased; they continue to dance in one's mind and whisper in one's ears.[52]

Denver also sings about how memories enable a person to love again. In "True Love Takes Time," he begins by expressing the impossibility of caring and giving again. Then, he says that it may take a miracle to dream again and remember how to live. Likewise, in "Perhaps Love," he states that the memories of love will bring one home and see him or her through. He concludes this song by singing about how his memories of love will be of his beloved.

There is a dark side to memories. Denver describes them as dark sands in "Islands" and as the lies told in the night in "The Game Is Over." When thinking about the winter in "Sticky Summer Weather," Denver acknowledges that his memories rage like a storm. Later in the song, he expresses the dark side of memories. He sings about a time when he remembered dreaming, but it is now gone.

Hard Times

Memories can serve to remind a person of the difficult times in his or her life, just like they remind Denver of loss and misfortune. In "Songs of . . . ," he calls hard times songs of the struggle. He sings about the hard times of living as being lost in the dark of misfortune in "Hold on Tightly," while he simple states that life is such a hard thing in "A Country Girl in Paris."

In "Alaska and Me," he sings about being raised in hard times, but, nevertheless, having a good life. He spends six lines in "Matthew," a ballad about one of his uncles, explaining what the phrase hard times means. Denver mentions lean years and a tornado that destroyed the farm—family, wheat crop, and home. In "To the Wild Country," Denver characterizes hard times as getting caught up in the struggle and the strain that accompanies

52. "True Love Takes Time."

living. He says that it feels like one has his or her back against a stone wall or like he or she has a finger in the dam that is ready to burst. The person is losing strength and going down. Likewise, in the chorus of "The Harder They Fall," Denver sings that some bad times cannot get worse. In fact, the bigger then are, the harder they fall. In the third verse of the song Denver characterizes hard times as like being caught between a rock and a hard place. It is feeling like one just can't win. Or, it's like one just can't recover from a slap in the face, he says.

Sometimes, hard times just mean the sorrow of life,[53] such as having lost the son of a sister in "African Sunrise." This was a child of love, a child of laughter, sings Denver in his sorrow. Similarly, love brings sorrow, as in "A Country Girl in Paris." Because she is three thousand miles away from the person she loves, her heart is filled with pain.

Alcohol

Another type of sorrow inflicted upon life is that which results from the abuse of alcohol. In three songs Denver sings about why people drink alcohol. He begins "Two Shots" with the typical equation that consumption of alcohol is necessary to have fun. In "Sleepin' Alone," Denver explains how some people in their loneliness turn to alcohol to solve their problems. He sings that sleeping alone can make a bottle one's dearest friend. In "Whiskey Basin Blues," the subject of the song is a lonely man in eastern Wyoming with a lady back in Laramie. He's spending the winter on his own in a drafty old cabin and drinking away his loneliness. Denver sings about moonshine, saying it is often thought of as a medicine for loneliness, but it leaves one with the blues. A passing reference is made to the misty taste of moonshine in "Take Me Home, Country Roads," but because of the ambiguity of the lyrics it is difficult to determine if Denver means liquor or the light of the moon!

Fear

Sometimes a person attempts to drown his or her sorrows in alcohol because of fear. Denver sings about all who live in fear in "Flying for Me." He specifies fear in "Love Again" as being afraid of the dark and the beat of his

---

53. "Zachary and Jennifer."

heart. He clarifies what he means when he sings that he was afraid that he might never love again. In "Rhymes and Reasons," he sings about the fear that is within him that seems to never end. Later, he identifies the endless fear as not knowing where a love-relationship is going.

Some people live lives in desperation in the fear of letting go, Denver sings in "It Amazes Me." In "Looking for Space," he contrasts this approach with his own fear of nothing changing. He sings that he is afraid that his life might reach a standstill.

Fear becomes the motivator for moral decision-making in "Raven's Child." The issue is the arms race with its nuclear warheads and lasers. Denver says that armaments are the result of fear, which chooses what is right and what is wrong. Denver believes that fear should not end in despair, however. He offers hope in "Never a Doubt." He sings about the things people fear; most fears mean nothing, he says. The sorrow and sadness can disappear.

In fact, in "Rocky Mountain High," he indicates that some fear is healthy. After singing about the man who finds himself in the mountains, he declares that his heart still knows a little fear of the things he still does not understand, like destroying the mountains and leaving scars on the land.

Forgiveness

Sometimes people live in fear because they do not forgive, says Denver. In various songs he emphasizes the importance of both expressing sorrow for having caused a hurt to another and receiving forgiveness from that person. Forgiveness removes blame, sings Denver in "Hold on Tightly." Likewise, in "Seasons of the Heart," he sings to the person he loved, who consequently left him, about not wanting to change because there is no one to blame. He explains that they no longer feel the same about each other.

In "I'm Sorry," Denver presents a litany of sorrow in order to seek the forgiveness of the one who went away. He says that he is sorry for the lies he told, for the things he did not say, and for taking many things for granted. Denver presents the idea of being sorry in "Whispering Jessie" as regrets. He sings about the things he would do differently, if he could do them again.

In "The Gift You Are," Denver tells his listeners about the prodigal son, an idea he alludes to in "What's on Your Mind," in which he sings about being lost and being found. The reference in both of these songs is to the parable of the prodigal son, which occurs uniquely in Luke's Gospel (15:11-32). This is a story about a younger son, who takes his share of his father's inheritance, leaves home, squanders it on indecent living, and returns home because he is starving. His father, who has been watching the road for him to reappear, forgives him for his loose living and accepts him back as his son with all his previous rights and privileges. Denver believes that this biblical story illustrates the unconditional aspect of, and the need for, forgiveness.

Escape

Denver, like all people, sometimes wants to escape from life, especially its problems. He expresses this in "Sail Away Home." However, his favorite way to sing about escape is through use of the metaphor flying. In "Fly Away," the chorus consists of three repetitions of fly away. Similarly, the chorus of "Cool an' Green an' Shady" is about finding a piece of grassy ground and lying down with one's eyes closed. Denver says that this gives a person the chance to find one's self or to lose one's self, while one's free spirit flies.

"Flying for Me," Denver's song dedicated to Challenger and her crew, begins with the idea that the astronauts were flying for everyone, since everybody would like to fly. Their literal escape from the earth's gravity signifies their escape from life to death and Denver's desire to escape life's problems.

No matter how much a person tries to escape from living, he or she is plunged back into it. Denver sings about this in the chorus of "I Can't Escape." He cannot escape thinking about his beloved, wishing she was still his, or thinking that he still loves her, caring for her.

Death

The journey of life, which is begun at birth, comes to an end with death. John Denver says that people want to live forever,[54] and after thinking about his lifetime he knows he will hate to see it end.[55] He becomes more realistic in "All of My Memories" when he says that he is looking for somewhere to

---

54. "Zachary and Jennifer."
55. "Poems, Prayers, and Promises."

lay down and die, while he adds a humorous note to the thought in "Around and Around;" he hopes to be around so he can be present when he dies!

Denver uses death as a metaphor in "Annie's Song" when he petitions her to let him die in her arms to indicate how much he loves her. The same metaphor is used in "Autograph" when Denver, wishing to regain the person he loved, says that he would be willing to die again. Also, in "I'm Sorry," Denver uses the death metaphor to indicate how he feels when talking to others about losing his beloved. He says that they know he is dying deep down inside.

In "Rocky Mountain Suite (Cold Nights in Canada)," he says that it is important to learn about other people, especially the ways that they lived and the ways that they died.

However, his best treatment of death is found in "On the Wings of a Dream." In this song, set in the context of a dream, Denver philosophizes about death. He sings about having a dream about dying, about being laid to rest, and then flying. This leads him to reflect that the only moment one really has is the present one. Denver then confronts the age-old question about why people are here and then gone. This ability to stand back, contemplate his life experiences, and celebrate his life enabled Denver to write "All This Joy," which aptly summarizes this chapter.

The first verse brings together joy, sorrow, promise, and pain. Denver declares that life, being, spirit, and love are just the way they are. In the succeeding verses, joy, sorrow, promise, and pain are predicated of the city and the world. Each becomes a city and a world of joy, sorrow, promise, and pain. However, Denver concludes that life, being, spirit, and love are just filled with joy, sorrow, promise, and pain. Again, for Denver this is the way that life simply is. This is the life that Denver says he celebrates.

Reflection

What aspects of your life do you celebrate? What things remind you of the changes that have occurred in your life? What trips have you taken that changed you? Whom have you loved during your life? How did the person(s) you loved change you? Of all the things you've done, what is your favorite memory? Explain.

5

Time as I've Known It

The title of this chapter comes from the opening line of "Around and Around," in which Denver states that time, as he has known it, does not take much time to pass by him. In fact, minutes quickly turn into days, into months, and into years. He continues this getting caught in the passing of time[1] idea in "Poems, Prayers, and Promises." He sings about days passing quickly and short nights. In "Songs of . . . ," he brings together in four lines the timely matter of what his songs consist. They are songs of the future, the past, the first day, and the last day. After presenting the idea that there should be no more hunger, no more killing, and no more wasting life away in "I Want to Live," Denver expresses the urgency of the time to act. He says that he knows that the idea's time has come. This chapter will explore Denver's songs about time in terms of yesterday, today, and tomorrow and morning, afternoon, and evening. Then, it will look at how he understands the changing of the seasons to be the visible manifestation of invisible time.

Yesterday

Denver's main theme concerning the day before today is stated in "Circus." He says that it is time to get out of yesterday. This line is preceded by his statement that it is time to find another way. He emphasizes the same idea in "To the Wild Country" when he sings about not living in yesterday. This is because yesterday is so very far away,[2] or as Denver exclaims in "Poems, Prayers, and Promises," yesterday is a long time ago. So, Denver concludes,

1. "What's on Your Mind."
2. "Anthem-Revelation."

78

people must move on. In "Sweet Surrender," he states that there is nothing behind and nothing that ties him to something that might have been true yesterday.

Today

Denver continues "Sweet Surrender" by saying that right now it seems to be more than enough to just be here today. For Denver, the moment at hand is the only thing one can really own.[3] It may be a lazy day, as in "Whiskey Basin Blues," but it is a brand new day,[4] the very first day.[5] Both of these later themes are united in "The Gift You Are" when Denver invites his listeners to make believe that today is the first day and everything is new. "You make the day the way it is, especially in your mind," states Denver.[6] Today is forever, he sings in "Rocky Mountain Suite (Cold Nights in Canada)."

In "Some Days Are Diamonds (Some Days Are Stone)," Denver compares good days to the sparkle of diamonds and bad days to the lackluster of stone. Some days, especially those full of love, are diamonds, while other days, those which seem long, are stone.[7] There are also a few days that may seem wrong.[8]

Singing about days that have gone soft and cloudy in "Fly Away," Denver attributes softness and cloudiness to loneliness. In other words, a person who is having a bad day is under the clouds or lonely. The best thing this individual can do is to fly away from the city.

Denver believes that every day should be celebrated. He says that "Anthem-Revelation" "is a song of celebration—a celebration of every new day, every new beginning, and every new moment. It's opportunity that's always there, that always needs to be created."[9] However, he prefers a daytime full of sun in "Druthers."

3. "On the Wings of a Dream."

4. "Season Suite: Spring."

5. "Anthem-Revelation."

6. Denver, *Anthology*, 128.

7. "Daydream."

8. "The Game Is Over."

9. Denver, *Anthology*, 26.

Tomorrow

Tomorrow, sings Denver in "Rocky Mountain Suite (Cold Nights in Canada," is just one of yesterday's dreams. He simply wonders about tomorrow in "Poems, Prayers, and Promises," and says there is nothing much to do tomorrow in "Whiskey Basin Blues." In "Sticky Summer Weather," he says that he has been trying to find a way to believe in tomorrow. But in "Sweet Surrender," he says that tomorrow is open and he does not know what the future holds. The same positivism is found in "The Eagle and the Hawk." Denver urges the listener to hope for the future. Likewise, in "60 Second Song for a Bank, With the Phrase 'May We Help You Today,'" he sings about seeing tomorrow in his dreams. Later in the song, he tells his listeners whose eyes can see tomorrow, though it might seem far away, that with some dreams to build on they can be helped today.

Denver spends more lyrics on tomorrow in "Take Me to Tomorrow" than in any other song. In this song he combines the negativism of trying to escape from the problems of today with the positivism of being open to the possibilities of the future. He sings about being taken to tomorrow, the day awaiting him, because that is where he would like to be.

Morning

Hazarding a guess, the morning is Denver's favorite time of the day. He mentions giving a voice to the dawn in "Wild Montana Skies." "Earth Day" begins with the call to celebrate the morning. Denver says that dreams are born in the dawn's early light. He connects the morning to birth and dreams in "You're So Beautiful" by singing about the person he loves, born on a quiet morning.

It makes no difference whether it is a snow crystal morning[10] or a misty one, as Denver describes in "Season Suite: Summer." He sings about the morning mist lying silently on the water. He also sings about the morning smiling like a superstar and being the promise of another sunny day.

Denver emphasizes his love for the morning in "Around and Around." He says that he loves to see the morning as it steals across the sky. Likewise, in "Anthem-Revelation," he urges his listeners to open their eyes, see the sunrise, and watch the morning come.

10. "The Gold and Beyond."

He turns his direct address into an invitation to remember how people long for the morning with dawn so far away in "The Gift You Are." He invites his listeners to remember the way that they long for morning's light. In "The Foxfire Suite: You Are," he pushes this idea one step further and says that the person he loves is every morning sunrise.

In "Like a Sad Song," he sings about how positive he is in the morning. He possesses a sense of belonging and an appreciation for everything beautiful. This is because in each morning there is the promise that someday one's true love will come, even though sometimes he might feel like it is a desperate morning, says Denver in "Never a Doubt." Denver says that he has always loved the promise of morning in "Whispering Jessie." It is with this great appreciation for the morning that in "Farewell Andromeda (Welcome to My Morning)," Denver welcomes his listeners to his morning, which he will craft into a perfect day.

Afternoon

Denver mentions the afternoon in only two songs. In "Back Home Again," he describes it as being heavy on his shoulders, while in "Cool an' Green an' Shady," he makes reference to easy afternoons.

Evening

Just as he enjoys the morning, when the night is gone,[11] so Denver enjoys the evening when daylight is leaving[12] or the darkest of nights,[13] as he refers to it. He says that he loves to see the sun go down in "Around and Around," and in "Eclipse," he says it takes a long time for the day to end with the sun fading in the western sky.

He attempts to photograph the evening in words in "You're So Beautiful" when he says that alpine meadows burn in the evening light, a reference to the pink glow reflected on the mountains and over the high country meadows by the setting sun and referred to as alpenglow. Similarly, when nighttime is rolling his way in "Song of Wyoming," Denver says that the sky

11. "Anthem-Revelation."
12. "Singing Skies and Dancing Waters."
13. "Love Is the Master."

looks like it is on fire and the light is slowly fading. Nevertheless, he adds that the day ends peaceful and still.

The same type of stillness is found in "Earth Day Every Day (Celebrate)." Denver invites the listener to celebrate evening and the stars that appear with the loss of the sun. Earlier in the same song he refers to the cry of a loon on a lake in the night. Denver enjoys being in the early evening chill.[14]

Spending a night or two all on his own[15] in the wilderness leads him to compare the experience to the delight of Annie in "Annie's Song." He begins the song by singing that she fills up his senses like a night in a forest.

However, when he is lonesome for the person he loves and thinks about her all night long,[16] he says that he cannot face the night alone. Similarly, in "I'm Sorry," he states that he cannot sleep at night. In "Fly Away," he sings about the effect of separation on the person he loves. He says that all of the nights he would have spent with her had gone sad and shady.

Sometimes it is just a restless mind that keeps Denver from getting to sleep at night. In "What's on Your Mind," he sings about being unable to quiet his heart or mind; so, he tosses and turns; he aches and burns.

For Denver the evening lends itself to loving and romance.[17] In "Druthers," he also characterizes the night as a time full of romance. He explains this in "Like a Sad Song," saying that the nighttime is the best time to tell his beloved that he loves her.

He summarizes his thoughts about the evening in "Farewell Andromeda (Welcome to My Morning)." Denver welcomes his listeners to his evening, tells them that he loves them, and thanks them for allowing him to enjoy the day.

Seasons Change

Denver's spirituality flows with the rhythm of the day, from morning to evening, and from yesterday through today to tomorrow. Likewise, the seasons affect him. Each individual season mirrors some aspect of his life. He explains that he loves the changing seasons in "60 Second Song for a Bank, With the Phrase 'May We Help You Today?'" In "Season Suite: Spring," he

14. "Seasons of the Heart."
15. "Poems, Prayers, and Promises."
16. "Daydream."
17. "A Country Girl in Paris."

asks his listeners if they can see themselves reflected in the seasons. Being in contact with the seasons is being in contact with one's own life. Denver sings about this in "Wild Montana Skies," a ballad about a man who grew up as an orphan but learned to be a farmer, to love the land, to read the seasons, and to make a stand.

Denver also uses the seasons to speak about differences between two people who have loved each other in "Seasons of the Heart." He explains that the differences are as natural as the seasons and the skies. However, in "Singing Skies and Dancing Waters," he says that because he was out of contact with the changes in the seasons, he took for granted the person who loved him and ended up losing his beloved. He sings that somehow he lost sight of seasons' tides rolling out and rolling in. A similar idea is expressed in "Joseph and Joe," a song about a priest and a cowboy. Denver sings about the seasons that drift between them.

Spring

Denver says that he has always loved springtime in "Whispering Jessie." He describes spring as manifesting itself with green leaves and the excitement of life reemerging. He explains that there is something about the country on the very first day of springtime in "Somethin' About." After a long winter, when springtime is rolling around slowly,[18] everyone is looking for signs of spring,[19] even if the only sign is the very first breath of spring.[20] Denver adds to the longing-for-spring idea in "Sticky Summer Weather." He says that it may seem like springtime was twenty years ago when the rain was sweet and the wind was cool and clean.

For Denver, spring is the season of birth. He expresses this best in "Season Suite: Spring." He tells his listeners to open their eyes to a new day, a clear blue sky, and a bright shining sun. They are to open their ears to hear the breeze declare that the winter cold and gray are gone. They are to open their hands to feel the spring rain. They are to taste the wind and smell the flowers. They are to open their mind and let the longer hours of daylight come in because the earth has been reborn.

With the connection between spring and the rebirth of the earth in the back of his mind, Denver places the birth of the hero in his ballad,

18. "Starwood in Aspen."
19. "Fly Away."
20. "The Gift You Are."

"Wild Montana Skies," in the spring. He describes it in the opening stanza of the song. He sings about the hero being born in the early morning rain when the geese were heading north again in the spring, when a warm wind from the south was bringing the first taste of spring.

When spring comes, all a person can do is sing about it. Denver sings about spring being alive in Carolina in "The Foxfire Suite: Spring is Alive." Then, he locates spring deep in the forest, high on a mountain, and down in a holler.

Summer

Denver has mixed emotions when it comes to summer. He says that he has always loved the long days of summer in "Whispering Jessie," and he says that his daughter, named Jennifer in his song, will sing in summer showers in "Zachary and Jennifer." But while he believes that summer is here to stay in "Season Suite: Summer," in "Sticky Summer Weather," he laments the season. He sings about sticky summer weather; it makes him feel like he is living under a blanket of humidity which inhibits his breathing. Furthermore, the days are like an oven, and the nights seem to last forever. In "Isabel," a dream-fantasy, he says that Isabel whispers of her sadness in the passing of the summer.

Fall

Denver sings about fall as his favorite time of the year in "What's on Your Mind." He mentions the changing colors, and says that early fall brings to mind August skies, lullabies, promises, dandelions, vines, clover, Aspen leaves shaking in the wind, and bees in "Cool an' Green an' Shady."

In "Season Suite: Fall," Denver says that the falling leaves whisper that winter is on its way. The falling leaves of the season become a metaphor for refugees in "Falling Leaves (The Refugees)." He dedicates the song to the refugees and compares them to falling leaves. He continues with his one wish for another spring and a blessing upon the falling leaves.

Denver's best presentation of fall is found in "Season Suite: Fall." He says that reflections on water remind him of passing days, nights, and time. He says that fall is the time to remember the warmth of yesterday. Then, he laments the end of summer and the beginning of fall. He sings about

September being swallowed by the wind and says that he is sad to see summer end and enter into the changing colors of fall.

Winter

Denver laments fall because it heralds the imminent coming of winter. He says that he cannot stand the thought of winter in "Sticky Summer Weather." He explains that he doesn't like winter because he has no fire and no one to keep him warm. The importance of a fire on a cold winter's night[21] is the topic of the second verse of "Season Suite: Winter." Denver sings about the fire that is slowly dying; it makes him feel like he cannot keep going.

The other depressing aspect of speaking about the coming of the winter[22] or the fact that winter's in the air[23] is the cold. In "Two Shots," a humorous song about hunting for ducks, Denver sings about a cold winter morning in a duck blind on a frozen river with snow falling and getting nothing but cold hands.

The cold is the topic of the first verse of "Season Suite: Winter." Denver sings about it being cold and getting even colder. He mentions the gray and white and winter everywhere and how as he gets older the snow gets him down. Likewise, in his dream-fantasy song, "Isabel," Denver says that Isabel is watching for the first soft snows of winter and the icy winds they bring.

Winter is the setting for only one complete song—"Whiskey Basin Blues." The ballad begins on a snow covered night in a drafty old cabin with a man spending the winter on his own and drowning his sorrows in moonshine. However, even in spite of Denver's dislike for winter, he finds one positive aspect to it in "Aspenglow." He sings about his chosen place to live. The winter days unfold and the hearts of the residents grow warmer with the cold.

Thus, yesterday turns into today, which becomes hope for tomorrow. Mornings move into afternoons and into evenings. The seasons—spring, summer, fall, and winter—change; they come and go. Even in the midst of winter depression, Denver can sing that it is worth waiting for another chance to see the summer sun.

21. "Alaska and Me."
22. "Rhymes and Reasons."
23. "Wrangell Mountain Song."

Reflection

Do you reflect more on the events of yesterday, those of today, or those of tomorrow? Explain. Which is your favorite time of the day: morning, afternoon, or evening? Why? Which is your favorite season: spring, summer, fall, or winter? How do the seasons of the year reflect the seasons of your life?

6

Share in the Freedom I Feel

Freedom

The title for this chapter comes from John Denver's "The Eagle and the Hawk," a song about the eagle, who lives in the high country, and the hawk, who, for those who believe in it, share in the freedom it feels when it flies. This general sense of freedom is also found in "Hold on Tightly," in which Denver sings about freedom that exists in the heart. In "One World," Denver also sings about freedom in this general sense. He says that he desires that everyone live in freedom.

Denver also sings about personal freedom. In "Higher Ground," he says that he has found the freedom which enables him to know that he will be reaching for higher ground. Likewise, as seen above in "One World," he says that he wants nothing for himself that he doesn't want for everyone, namely, to live in freedom.

In "Let Us Begin (What Are We Making Weapons for?)," he sings about not being personally free. He says that he feels like a prisoner, like a slave to the powers that be, while in "Anthem-Revelation," he says that he is just learning how it feels to be free. In "Song of Wyoming," he sings about waking up on the range and feeling so free that he could fly. Of personal freedom Denver says that he wanted to free himself and join himself with it.[1]

Personal freedom is glimpsed from wildness or wilderness freedom, according to Denver in "American Child." Denver sings about Alaska and the pioneer life that many people there still live. Such a life requires courage and strength to survive, but it is a place where one can be free.

1. "Flying for Me."

Freedom defined as wildness or wilderness for Denver occurs in a number of songs. In "Earth Day Every Day (Celebrate)," he sings about freedom that flies to the call of the wild. In "To the Wild Country," he calls it freedom on the run, and in "Calypso" he names it as free as a wind-swell. He returns to the idea of the experience of freedom's wildness as being on the open range, as found in "Song of Wyoming." In "I'd Rather Be a Cowboy," he sings about riding the range. Such freedom gets more specified in "Eagles and Horses." Denver sings about the horses running in freedom. Likewise, the eagles know no limits or boundaries; they are free, too.

Denver best summarizes this sense of wildness or wilderness freedom in "To the Wild Country." He can hear Alaska's spirit calling him, he says, to the wild country where he belongs.

Besides general, personal, and wildness/wilderness freedom, Denver also sings about patriotic freedom. In "The Foxfire Suite: Spring Is Alive," he sings about a hundred years ago, when people came to Carolina seeking independence. While living in the land of the free, Denver sings about the responsibility that people have to defend the freedom of their country in "Let Us Begin (What Are We Making Weapons for?)." The person in the song returns from war after serving his or her country and defending freedom. Denver explains what results when people want freedom by referring to the crumbling of the Berlin Wall in "Raven's Child." He sings about walls that fall because people yearn to be free. In the same song, he says that it is important to keep vigil for freedom.

Peace

The result of freedom—general, personal, wildness/wilderness, and patriotic—is peace, says Denver. In his songs he begins with peace between two people. In "Thanks to You," Denver offers thanks to another because she helped him find peace within himself. Likewise in "The Foxfire Suite: You Are," he says that the other is how the peace begins.

In "Hold on Tightly," he locates the beginning of peace in the heart. First, he asks about the peace for which people long. Then, in the chorus he answers his question by singing that it is found in the heart.

Denver says that he wants to work in peace,[2] that he wants peace of mind,[3] like that found in Aspen, and he wants it to be a peace beyond all

2. "One World."
3. "Aspenglow."

fear.[4] His only concretization of peace is found in "Goodbye Again" in which he sings about lying by the side of the person he loves and finding the greatest peace he's ever known.

If peace is one's vision, says Denver in "Let Us Begin (What Are We Making Weapons for?)," then one should begin to make peace. In "Autograph," he says that peace on earth is the only way.

The one picture that he paints of peace on earth is found in "Children of the Universe" and is borrowed from the book of the prophet Isaiah. Denver sings about the hawk flying with the mourning dove and the lion lying with the sheep. Denver's echo of the prophet Isaiah comes from the following verses:

> The wolf shall live with the lamb, the leopard shall lie down with the kid, the calf and the lion and the fatling together, and a little child shall lead them. The cow and the bear shall graze, their young shall lie down together; and the lion shall eat straw like the ox. They will not hurt or destroy on all my holy mountain; for the earth will be full of the knowledge of the LORD, as the waters cover the sea. (Isa 11:6-7, 9)

War

Of course Isaiah's photograph of nature's natural enemies in peaceful coexistence is an idyllic vision. The fact of the matter is that people do not always get along, and the result is war. Denver sings about his dislike for war, but he also knows that sometimes it is necessary to go to war to protect freedom and peace.

In "Wrangell Mountain Song," he sings about being three years from the war and having served his country well. The *you* of "The Foxfire Suite: You Are" is why the war is over.

In three songs Denver condemns the arms race which leads to war. In "Raven's Child," he sings about the armament king who sits on his arrogant throne. Denver says that it is the arms trade with its nuclear warheads and lasers which now decide what is right and what is wrong in the world. He is more explicit about arms in "Sail Away Home." He says that he cannot take the guns anymore because they result in screams and pain. The arms trade has got to stop, sings Denver. His dislike for war is found most strongly

4. "Falling Leaves (The Refugees)."

in "Let Us Begin (What Are We Making Weapons for?)," a ballad about a family which loses many members to death in war. Denver sings about giving up a father to South Korea and his brother's mind to Vietnam. In the chorus he asks about why people make weapons and keep feeding the war machine. The second verse tells more about the hardships of war. Denver sings about a soldier-son, who was like his father. He gave his life in a revolution. In the third verse Denver asks the listeners to remember all the lives that have been lost in wars. Then, he says that people could make the last war the last one ever fought if peace becomes their vision.

In Denver's music, general, personal, wildness/wilderness, and patriotic freedom result in peace. The opposite of peace is war, which is often fueled by the arms race. According to Denver, the way to end war is to make peace one's personal vision.

Reflection

What is your definition of freedom? Is there an animal you associate with freedom, like Denver does? How does Denver echo your understanding of peace? war? Do you think he's right about peace and war? Explain.

7

I Can Hear Her Spirit Calling Me

Alaska

The title for this chapter is a line from "To the Wild Country." While Alaska is one of John Denver's favorite spots on the earth, he sings about many of the places which he has visited and those which he loves. Sometimes he just mentions a place in the song or in its title, such as in "One World" which mentions New York City and Tokyo. At other times he dedicates a whole song to a place, such as "Alaska and Me." In the chorus of this song he salutes the forty-ninth state and toasts Alaska and the people who live there; also, he toasts the wilderness and the freedom that can be found there.

All totaled, Denver has four songs dedicated to Alaska. In "Alaska and Me," he says that as a child living in the city he dreamed of Alaska and flying over the mountains and glaciers there. The ballad continues with him growing up and going to school and, finally, moving to Alaska. Denver concludes this song with a desire once more to gaze at the great Northern Lights. Then, he gives a final salute to Alaska's beauty.

In "American Child," a song about getting in contact with the wildness and spiritual freedom within himself, Denver says that the place to do this is Alaska. He sings about Alaska as the land of the midnight sun where the whale and the polar bear run on the icy, blue Arctic Ocean. He also mentions the pioneer life with its requisite courage and strength needed to survive.

As stated above, Denver mentions Alaska in "To the Wild Country." This song, like "American Child," is about finding one's self. Denver says that when he is in civilization, his heart turns to Alaska, where there is freedom. Alaska's spirit calls him, he sings.

In "Wrangell Mountain Song," the first verse deals with Alaska in general, while the chorus is about one of the mountain ranges in the state—the Wrangell Mountains. Denver aptly describes the rainy climate in Alaska and how for seven days there has been no sunshine. Bush pilots fly low and use the shoreline for guidance since they cannot use landmarks. Nevertheless, Denver says that he cannot wait to see the Wrangell Mountains.

On the *Autograph* album cover, Denver writes, "The Alaska songs are dedicated to all the people in Alaska: . . . the Eskimos, Aleuts, and all the men and women who emigrated from the Lower Forty-Eight to make that wild place their home. I salute you."

Colorado

Two of Denver's songs mention the state in which he lived: Colorado. One is found in "Rocky Mountain High," Denver's signature song. In the chorus of this song Denver sings about the Colorado Rocky Mountain high. He sings about the lightning, which he calls fire in the sky; lightning is an element of biblical theophanies.[1] He sings about the soft starlight in the mountains. When the chorus is repeated three times throughout the song, Denver attributes more to Colorado, as the third line is subsequently changed to talking to God and listening to the casual reply—a biblical reference to Moses' encounter with God on Mount Sinai (Horeb) in which Moses spoke to God and he answered him with thunder (Exod 19:19). The last time the chorus is sung the third line is about being poor if one never saw an eagle fly or joined friends around a campfire where everybody is high.

The other reference to the state of Colorado in Denver's music is found in "Whispering Jessie." In describing himself, Denver depicts himself as old cowboy from high Colorado. The song is about Jessie, who is physically gone but still lives in Denver's heart.

Montana

"Wild Montana Skies" is a ballad which explains how a man grew up, learned how to be a farmer, left the land, and then returned. The chorus

---

1. Boyer, *Divine Presence*, 52–4.

consists of Denver's directions to the state of Montana concerning the care of this person. He tells Montana to give him a home, the love of a good family, a wife, a fire in his heart, a light in his eyes, the wild wind for a brother, and the wild Montana skies. The state of Montana is also mentioned in "Hitchhiker," another ballad-like piece about an old man holding out his thumb in the wind. As the old hitchhiker tells his story about being a barker in a circus, he says that he was headed for Montana when he hired a dancer. He, of course, falls in love with her, but she departs. The old man wishes that she were with him now, as he continues his thirty years as a hitchhiker.

Wyoming

Denver dedicated two songs to the state of Wyoming. One of them, "Song of Wyoming," is about the freedom experienced out on the plains. In the last half of the first verse Denver sings about hearing night birds calling on a trail and the wind whispering through the cottonwood trees in the canyon. He refers to these phenomena as Wyoming's song for him. He concludes the second verse with a similar refrain, mentioning a coyote's howl. And the final verse echoes the first two in which he mentions the wind singing through the sage brush.

The other song dedicated to Wyoming is set in Whiskey Basin and appropriately titled "Whisky Basin Blues." It is about a man all alone on a snow covered night in eastern Wyoming. He has a lady in Laramie, but he is spending the winter on his own, filling his cup with moonshine, and drinking his loneliness away.

Other States

Besides singing about Alaska, Colorado, Montana, and Wyoming, Denver mentions other states in various songs. In "Take Me Home, Country Roads," not only is West Virginia mentioned, but so are her Blue Ridge Mountains and Shenandoah River. Denver calls West Virginia a mountain mamma.

Western Oklahoma is the setting for "Let us Begin (What Are We Making Weapons for?)," Denver's ballad about a man whose father, brother, and son were involved in various wars and who was suffering from foreclosure on his farm.

In "Matthew," another ballad, Denver sings about his uncle who was born just south of Colby, Kansas. He describes gold as a windy Kansas wheat field and blue as the Kansas summer sky. For his uncle, who grew up a Kansas farm boy, life was mostly having fun until a series of natural disasters forced him to leave the farm and live with Denver's family.

Denver uses the first section of "The Foxfire Suite: Spring Is Alive" to salute the Carolinas. The chorus begins by announcing spring in Carolina. In the first verse he traces the over-one-hundred-year history of those who came to Carolina from far across the water. Then he sings about their courage coming there to seek independence. He adds that they found the Smoky Mountains.

Denver mentions Tennessee in "A Country Girl in Paris." This song is about the sadness experienced by a woman living in Paris. Her memories of Nashville, Tennessee, in the rain center on a country boy three thousand miles away. Denver laments the difficulties of performing in Nashville in "Country Love." He sings about Nashville tears, Nashville hearts, and Nashville nights and the loneliness, brokenness, and lack of happiness of a Nashville superstar.

Various Cities

Denver mentions the city in which he lives—Aspen—in three songs. In "Starwood in Aspen," a tribute to his home, which he named "Starwood," he sings about the distance involved in traveling from one performance to the next. He says that it is a long way home to Starwood in Aspen. He calls Starwood his sweet Rocky Mountain paradise.

He dedicated "Aspenglow" to Aspen's residents, who "have a celebration every year called Winterskol, and each year it has a theme." Denver says, "The first winter I was working in Aspen, the theme was Aspenglow." The people "talk about 'taking on an Aspenglow,' the connotation being that somehow just living here brings on a glow that shows the effect of this little town on your life."[2]

In "Aspenglow" Denver attempts to describe this phenomenon: "Aspenglow is a sense of family, of living here, of being able to appreciate the little subtleties which are so often missed; sunlight through the pine, the warmth of winter wine, sitting down and having a glass of wine with someone at a picnic on the side of a mountain. All of a sudden that little sharing of the cup can mean a whole lot of things."[3]

2. Denver, *Anthology*, 25.
3. Ibid.

Denver sets "The Harder They Fall" in Aspen, Colorado, on a Saturday night. The main character in the song is Jessie, who is caught between a rock and a hard place. She wishes she were home, but she is afraid of being alone.

The city of Denver gets mentioned in "Starwood in Aspen" as well as Los Angeles. It is a long way from Los Angeles, California, to Denver, Colorado, sings Denver, emphasizing both the distance from his home and how much he hates to be away from it. He also mentions Los Angeles in "I'd Rather Be a Cowboy (Lady's Chains)," a song about Jessie, who left the country behind and moved to the city. Denver sings that living near a Los Angeles freeway is not his kind of having fun!

The city of Paris, France, is mentioned a number of times in "A Country Girl in Paris." The subject of the song, a country girl in Paris, sees the moonlight reflected on the River Seine while walking along the Champs Elysees, but her heart is filled with pain. She is dreaming about her lover in Nashville.

Other Countries

Besides the states and cities that Denver has visited around the United States, he has traveled abroad. Some of the names of these countries and their cities have made it into his songs. Among these is Australia.

Denver dedicates an entire song, "Sing Australia," to this country. He begins by explaining why he went to Australia. He went there to see the koala, the kangaroo, and to hear an aborigine play a didgeridoo, among other things. Then he narrates some of the history of the country, namely, as a penal colony visited by British royalty. The chorus explains where Denver hears Australia's song: in the desert, in the cities, in the mountains, in the sea, in the stories, and in the people who live there. After mentioning some of Australia's famous people, such as waltzing Matilda and Crocodile Dundee, Denver returns to his history theme marking Australia's two hundredth anniversary. He concludes the song by exhorting all to sing of Australia four times. Then, he adds that in the sands of Sydney Harbor, he can hear Australia sing.

Denver mentions the country of Africa in "African Sunrise," a song about hope for the end of a drought in that country and, consequently, an end to starvation. At the beginning of the song Denver sings about the

African sunrise shining and smiling on a new day. Later in the song, he sings about the African sunrise as light of a new day.

Denver's song, "Amazon (Let This Be a Voice)," bears the name of the famous river on the African continent, but he philosophizes that the river that runs from the mountains is all rivers and all rivers are that one. Later in the song he identifies it as the river of no regret.

Two songs are set in China. One of them, "Shanghai Breezes," is Denver's lament about being separated from the person he loves. However, he remembers that the same moon and stars in the sky are seen no matter where a person is on the earth. He can hear the voice of his beloved in the breezes in old Shanghai. Later in the song, he says that Shanghai breezes, which are cool and clearing and evening's sweet caress, are also soft and gentle and remind him of his lover's tenderness.

The other song set in China is "Heart to Heart," in which Denver mentions Hong Kong. Again, he is lamenting that he is far away from the person he loves. He sings about sitting in old Hong Kong and seeing the harbor lights looking like diamonds in the sky.

In two other songs Denver mentions China. In "I'm Sorry," he tells the person who has left him that he is sorry for the way things are in China. In "Sleepin' Alone," he sings that all the tea in China will not make a house a home.

The country of India gets a passing mention in the opening line of "It's About Time." Denver sings about a full moon over India and Gandhi living again.

Likewise, both the country of Canada and its city, Jasper, Alberta, are mentioned in "Rocky Mountain Suite (Cold Nights in Canada)." Denver sets the song in a meadow in Jasper, Alberta, and then later sings about the cold nights in Canada and icy blue winds.

Like India and Canada, Mexico gets a passing reference in "Circus." After Denver discovers that he has been looking everywhere but going nowhere, he sings about maybe trying the circus or going back to Mexico.

Rocky Mountains

In comparison to states, cities, and other countries, the Rocky Mountains are referred to the most in Denver's lyrics. In this area, Denver's best known song is "Rocky Mountain High." While the piece is a ballad about a man finding himself in the high country, it is also a description of what it is like to experience the Rocky Mountains. Such an experience involves climbing cathedral mountains and seeing silver clouds. It entails walking in quiet solitude in the forests and along the streams, as well as trying to understand the serenity of a clear, blue mountain lake.

The Rocky Mountain high can be caused by watching it rain fire—lightning—in the sky or observing how starlight shadow is softer than a lullaby. Sometimes it is caused by talking to God and listening to the casual reply, knowing that one would be poor if he or she never saw an eagle fly, or by friends sitting around a campfire and getting high! In "Annie's Other Song," Denver sings about the solitude he finds in the Rocky Mountains. While riding a horse in the Rocky Mountains, he enjoys the quiet, the peace, and the stars.

The Rockies are living, sings Denver in "Rocky Mountain Suite (Cold Nights in Canada;" never will they die. They provide him with Rocky Mountain memories[4] and a setting for his home, a Rocky Mountain paradise.[5]

Only in "Love Is the Master" does Denver mention the San Juan Mountains, one range within the Rocky Mountain chain in Colorado. He says that he was riding with friends and telling stories around a camp fire.

It is interesting to note that the Spirit seems to call Denver out of the city and into the country which he loves. After visiting either a new or an old place, the experience sparked him to write a song about it. The country represents freedom for Denver, while the city reminds him of loneliness. In both cases, Denver's is a lived spirituality based on countless experiences, many of them recorded forever in the lyrics of his songs.

Reflection

Where is your favorite place on the earth? Does that place call you to it? How does that place nourish your spirit?

4. "Trade Winds."
5. "Starwood in Aspen."

Conclusion

J ohn Denver, trained architect, international performer, was a man who sang about his experiences of living, and, in doing so, revealed his spirituality. His music styles consisted of ballads, country/western, jazz, rock, bluegrass, and love songs. Some of his music was neo-romantic, an attempt to capture in poetry and music the sights, sounds, tastes, touches, and smells of a lifetime of experiences. Denver died at the age of fifty-three in a solo airplane crash.

Through the lyrics of his songs, Denver revealed his spirituality, that invisible force which motivated or inspired his personal spirit and gave insight and meaning to what he did and why he did it. Spirituality, for Denver, was that energy which filled the sails of his soul and propelled him throughout his life.

The same or similar themes emerge from many of his songs. Denver believed that people are not alone in the world; the divine presence—no matter what name one uses to identify it—is always with them. This theme was explored in chapter 1 using the subtitles of solitude, faith, prayer, grace, and spirit/wind.

Denver had a great respect for mother earth, which provides for the needs of all her children. Chapter 2 explored Denver's understanding of mother earth and all her elements: the sun, the moon, the stars and sky, clouds, the rainbow, storms and lightning, snow, mountains, forests, deserts, canyons, prairies, flowers, water, animals/wildlife, and, the most important, respect for the earth.

Denver's spirituality encompassed everything and everyone. He saw the universe as one, and he worked to bring people together rather than see them divided. This theme was explored in chapter 3 under the subtitles of country/city, home, wife/family, children, and, Denver's vision that all are one.

Chapter 4 presented the subject of celebrating life. Denver counted every day as an opportunity to joyously experience living. The themes he sang about included birth, journey, questions and answers, living, experiences, changes, self-discovery, growing old, dreams, falling into love, falling out of love, loneliness, service, joy, magic, memories, hard times, alcohol, fear, forgiveness, escape, and death.

People celebrate living in a construct called time. Denver sang about time in terms of yesterday, today, and tomorrow. Those themes were explored in chapter 5 along with morning, afternoon, and evening. Likewise, the change in seasons from winter to spring, from spring to summer, from summer to fall, and from fall to winter are presented in many of Denver's songs.

Freedom was a very important concept for Denver. Many of his songs explore the meaning of the word. Chapter 6 examined the various ways Denver defined freedom along with his great desire for peace and his anti-war stance.

The last chapter focused on how Denver was called by the Spirit to various places on the third planet from the sun. Chapter 7 presented his experiences in the states of Alaska, Colorado, Montana, Wyoming, and others. It also presented various cities and other countries that inspired him to write songs. However, when all is said and done, the Rocky Mountains have a special place in Denver's spirituality, and that is seen in the countless references to them in his songs.

Denver's signature song, "Rocky Mountain High," is a ballad about a twenty-seven-year-old man getting in touch with his spirit in the mountains. However, it is also a song about the force which inspires one's spirit—God, who is revealed through a lifetime of experiences. Denver's spirituality was a lifetime of seeking grace, seeking God, with every step at every time and in every place. Through the lyrics of his music, Denver shared with the listener how he did that: He talked to God and listened to the casual reply. That line from "Rocky Mountain High" aptly captures the Spirit and the spirit that animated John Denver for fifty-three years.

Denver was not religious in the usual sense of the term, such as being devoted to a particular set of beliefs or belonging to a particular ecclesial denomination. However, anyone who can sing about God's presence, mother earth, world unity, celebrating life, time, freedom, and mystical experiences is certainly a spiritual person. Anyone who sings about seeking grace and Christ on the cross burning with desire—from "Stonehaven Sunset"—had some spiritual dimension to his life. The writer hopes that the reader has enjoyed this thematic analysis of John Denver's music and has come to experience his spirituality.

Reflection

What is your favorite John Denver song? What spiritual experience does it articulate for you? How does Denver's music nourish your spirituality? Explain.

Bibliography and Discography

Boyer, Mark G. *An Abecedarian of Animal Spirit Guides: Spiritual Growth through Reflections on Creatures.* Eugene, OR: Wipf and Stock, 2016.

———. *Divine Presence: Elements of Biblical Theophanies.* Eugene, OR: Wipf and Stock, 2017.

———. "Seeking Grace with Every Step": The Spirituality of John Denver. Springfield, MO: Leavenhouse Publications, 1996.

Denver, John. "A Country Girl in Paris." *Higher Ground.* Windstar D4-72850, 1988, Cassette Tape.

———. "African Sunrise." *Dreamland Express.* RCA AFL1-5458, 1985, Long Playing Record.

———. "Alaska and Me." *Higher Ground.* Windstar D4-72850, 1988, Cassette Tape.

———. "All of My Memories." *Aerie.* RCA LSP-4607, 1971, Long Playing Record.

———. "All This Joy." *Higher Ground.* Windstar D4-72850, 1988, Cassette Tape.

———. "Amazon (Let This Be a Voice)." *Different Directions.* Windstar WR-58888-4, 1991, Cassette Tape.

———. "American Child." *Autograph.* RCA AQL1-3449, 1980, Long Playing Record.

———. "Ancient Rhymes." *The Flower That Shattered the Stone*. Windstar WR-5-3334-4, 1990, Cassette Tape.

———. "Annie's Other Song." *An Evening with John Denver*. RCA PL2-0764, Long Playing Record.

———. "Annie's Song." *Back Home Again*. RCA CPL1-0548, 1974, Long Playing Record.

———. "Anthem-Revelation." *Take Me to Tomorrow*. RCA LSP-4278,970, Long Playing Record.

———. *Anthology*. Edited by Milton Okun. Port Chester, NY: Cherry Lane Music, 1982.

———. "Around and Around." *Poems, Prayers, and Promises*. RCA LSP-4499, 1971, Long Playing Record.

———. "Aspenglow." *Take Me to Tomorrow*. RCA LSP-4278,970, Long Playing Record.

———. "Autograph." *Autograph*. RCA AQL1-3449, 1980, Long Playing Record.

———. "A Wild Heart Looking for a Home." *Dreamland Express*. RCA AFL1-5458, 1985, Long Playing Record.

———. "Back Home Again." *Back Home Again*. RCA CPL1-0548, 1974, Long Playing Record.

———. "Calypso." *Windsong*. RCA APL1-1183, 1975, Long Playing Record.

———. "Children of the Universe." *Seasons of the Heart*. RCA AFL1-4256, 1981-1982, Long Playing Record.

———. "Circus." *Rhymes and Reasons*. RCA LSP-4207, 1969, Long Playing Record.

———. "Come and Let Me Look in Your Eyes." *Spirit*. RCA APL1-1694, 1976, Long Playing Record.

———. "Cool an' Green an' Shady." *Back Home Again*. RCA CPL1-0548, 1974, Long Playing Record.

———. "Country Love." *Some Days Are Diamonds*. RCA AFL1-4055, 1981, Long Playing Record.

———. "Dancing with the Mountains." *Autograph*. RCA AQL1-3449, 1980, Long Playing Record.

———. "Daydream." *Rhymes and Reasons*. RCA LSP-4207, 1969, Long Playing Record.

———. "Deal with the Ladies." *Higher Ground*. Windstar D4-72850, 1988, Cassette Tape.

———. "Downhill Stuff." *J.D. (John Denver)*. RCA AQL1-3075, 1979, Long Playing Record.

———. "Dreamland Express." *Dreamland Express*. RCA AFL1-5458, 1985, Long Playing Record.

———. "Druthers." *I Want to Live*. RCA AFL1-2521, 1977, Long Playing Record.

———. "The Eagle and the Hawk." *Aerie*. RCA LSP-4607, 1971, Long Playing Record.

———. "Eagles and Horese (I'm Flying Again)." *The Flower That Shattered the Stone*. Windstar WR-5-3334-4, 1990, Cassette Tape.

———. "Earth Day Every Day (Celebrate)." *Earth Songs*. Windstar WR-53333-4, 1990, Cassette Tape.

———. "Eclipse." *Back Home Again*. RCA CPL1-0548, 1974, Long Playing Record.

———. "Falling Leaves (The Refugees)." *Higher Ground*. Windstar D4-72850, 1988, Cassette Tape.

———. "Falling out of Love." *It's About Time*. RCA AFL1-4683, 1983, Long Playing Record.

———. "Farwell Andromeda (Welcome to My Morning)." *Farewell Andromeda*. RCA APL1-0101, 1973, Long Playing Record.

————. "Flight (The Higher We Fly)." *It's About Time*. RCA AFL1-4683, 1983, Long Playing Record.

————. "Fly Away." *Windsong*. RCA APL1-1183, 1975, Long Playing Record.

————. "Flying for Me." *One World*. RCA AFL1-5811, 1986, Long Playing Record.

————. "Follow Me." *Take Me to Tomorrow*. RCA LSP-4278,970, Long Playing Record.

————. "For Baby (For Bobbie)." *Rocky Mountain High*. RCA LSP-4731, 1972, Long Playing Record.

————. "For You." *Higher Ground*. Windstar D4-72850, 1988, Cassette Tape.

————. "The Foxfire Suite: Spring Is Alive." *Different Directions*. Windstar WR-58888-4, 1991, Cassette Tape.

————. "The Foxfire Suite: You Are." *Different Directions*. Windstar WR-58888-4, 1991, Cassette Tape.

————. "The Foxfire Suite: Whisper the Wind." *Different Directions*. Windstar WR-58888-4, 1991, Cassette Tape.

————. "The Game Is Over." *Whose Garden Was This*. RCA LSP-4414, 1970, Long Playing Record.

————. "The Gift You Are." *The Flower That Shattered the Stone*. Windstar WR-5-3334-4, 1990, Cassette Tape.

————. "The Gold and Beyond." *John Denver's Greatest Hits: Volume 3*. RCA AJL1-5313, 1984, Long Playing Record.

————. "Goodbye Again." *Rocky Mountain High*. RCA LSP-4731, 1972, Long Playing Record.

————. "The Harder They Fall." *Dreamland Express*. RCA AFL1-5458, 1985, Long Playing Record.

————. "Heart to Heart." *Seasons of the Heart*. RCA AFL1-4256, 1981-1982, Long Playing Record.

————. "Hey There, Mr. Lonely Heart." *One World*. RCA AFL1-5811, 1986, Long Playing Record.

————. "Higher Ground." *Higher Ground*. Windstar D4-72850, 1988, Cassette Tape.

————. "Hitchhiker." *Spirit*. RCA APL1-1694, 1976, Long Playing Record.

————. "Hold on Tightly." *It's About Time*. RCA AFL1-4683, 1983, Long Playing Record.

————. "How Can I Leave You Again." *I Want to Live*. RCA AFL1-2521, 1977, Long Playing Record.

————. "I Can't Escape." *One World*. RCA AFL1-5811, 1986, Long Playing Record.

————. "I'd Rather Be a Cowboy (Lady's Chains)." *Farewell Andromeda*. RCA APL1-0101, 1973, Long Playing Record.

————. "I'm Sorry." *Windsong*. RCA APL1-1183, 1975, Long Playing Record.

————. "In My Heart." *Autograph*. RCA AQL1-3449, 1980, Long Playing Record.

————. "I Remember Romance." *It's About Time*. RCA AFL1-4683, 1983, Long Playing Record.

————. "Isabel." *Take Me to Tomorrow*. RCA LSP-4278,970, Long Playing Record.

————. "Islands." *Seasons of the Heart*. RCA AFL1-4256, 1981-1982, Long Playing Record.

————. "It Amazes Me." *I Want to Live*. RCA AFL1-2521, 1977, Long Playing Record.

————. "It Makes Me Giggle." *Spirit*. RCA APL1-1694, 1976, Long Playing Record.

————. "It's About Time." *It's About Time*. RCA AFL1-4683, 1983, Long Playing Record.

————. "It's a Possibility." *One World*. RCA AFL1-5811, 1986, Long Playing Record.

————. "I Want to Live." *I Want to Live*. RCA AFL1-2521, 1977, Long Playing Record.

———. "I Wish I Could Have Been There (Woodstock)." *Whose Garden Was This*. RCA LSP-4414, 1970, Long Playing Record.

———. "Joseph and Joe." *J.D. (John Denver)*. RCA AQL1-3075, 1979, Long Playing Record.

———. "Leaving on a Jet Plane." *Rhymes and Reasons*. RCA LSP-4207, 1969, Long Playing Record.

———. "Let Us Begin (What Are We Making Weapons for?)." *One World*. RCA AFL1-5811, 1986, Long Playing Record.

———. "Life Is So Good." *J.D. (John Denver)*. RCA AQL1-3075, 1979, Long Playing Record.

———. "Like a Sad Song." *Spirit*. RCA APL1-1694, 1976, Long Playing Record.

———. "Looking for Space." *Windsong*. RCA APL1-1183, 1975, Long Playing Record.

———. "Love Again." *One World*. RCA AFL1-5811, 1986, Long Playing Record.

———. "Love Is Everywhere." *Windsong*. RCA APL1-1183, 1975, Long Playing Record.

———. "Love Is the Master." *One World*. RCA AFL1-5811, 1986, Long Playing Record.

———. "Matthew." *Back Home Again*. RCA CPL1-0548, 1974, Long Playing Record.

———. "The Music Is You." *Back Home Again*. RCA CPL1-0548, 1974, Long Playing Record.

———. "My Sweet Lady." *Poems, Prayers, and Promises*. RCA LSP-4499, 1971, Long Playing Record.

———. "Never a Doubt." *Higher Ground*. Windstar D4-72850, 1988, Cassette Tape.

———. "One World." *One World*. RCA AFL1-5811, 1986, Long Playing Record.

———. "On the Wings of a Dream." *It's About Time*. RCA AFL1-4683, 1983, Long Playing Record.

———. "Opposite Tables." *Seasons of the Heart*. RCA AFL1-4256, 1981-1982, Long Playing Record.

———. "Perhaps Love." *Seasons of the Heart*. RCA AFL1-4256, 1981-1982, Long Playing Record.

———. "Poems, Prayers, and Promises." *Poems, Prayers, and Promises*. RCA LSP-4499, 1971, Long Playing Record.

———. "Prisoners (Hard Life, Hard Times)." *Rocky Mountain High*. RCA LSP-4731, 1972, Long Playing Record.

———. "Raven's Child." *The Flower That Shattered the Stone*. Windstar WR-5-3334-4, 1990, Cassette Tape.

———. "Rhymes and Reasons." *Rhymes and Reasons*. RCA LSP-4207, 1969, Long Playing Record.

———. "Rocky Mountain High." *Rocky Mountain High*. RCA LSP-4731, 1972, Long Playing Record.

———. "Rocky Mountain Suite (Cold Nights in Canada)." *Farewell Andromeda*. RCA APL1-0101, 1973, Long Playing Record.

———. "Sail Away Home." *Whose Garden Was This*. RCA LSP-4414, 1970, Long Playing Record.

———. "Seasons of the Heart." *Seasons of the Heart*. RCA AFL1-4256, 1981-1982, Long Playing Record.

———. "Season Suite: Fall." *Rocky Mountain High*. RCA LSP-4731, 1972, Long Playing Record.

———. "Season Suite: Spring." *Rocky Mountain High*. RCA LSP-4731, 1972, Long Playing Record.

———. "Season Suite: Summer." *Rocky Mountain High*. RCA LSP-4731, 1972, Long Playing Record.

———. "Season Suite: Winter." *Rocky Mountain High*. RCA LSP-4731, 1972, Long Playing Record.

———. "Shanghai Breezes." *Seasons of the Heart*. RCA AFL1-4256, 1981-1982, Long Playing Record.

———. "Sing Australia." *Higher Ground*. Windstar D4-72850, 1988, Cassette Tape.

———. "Singing Skies and Dancing Waters." *I Want to Live*. RCA AFL1-2521, 1977, Long Playing Record.

———. "60 Second Song for a Bank, with the Phrase 'May We Help You Today?'" *Aerie*. RCA LSP-4607, 1971, Long Playing Record.

———. "Sleepin' Alone." *Some Days Are Diamonds*. RCA AFL1-4055, 1981, Long Playing Record.

———. "Some Days Are Diamonds (Some Days Are Stone)." *Some Days Are Diamonds*. RCA AFL1-4055, 1981, Long Playing Record.

———. "Somethin' About." *It's About Time*. RCA AFL1-4683, 1983, Long Playing Record.

———. "Song of Wyoming." *Windsong*. RCA APL1-1183, 1975, Long Playing Record.

———. "Songs of . . . ." *J.D. (John Denver)*. RCA AQL1-3075, 1979, Long Playing Record.

———. "Spirit." *Windsong*. RCA APL1-1183, 1975, Long Playing Record.

———. "Starwood in Aspen." *Aerie*. RCA LSP-4607, 1971, Long Playing Record.

———. "Sticky Summer Weather." *Take Me to Tomorrow*. RCA LSP-4278,970, Long Playing Record.

———. "Stonehaven Sunset." *The Flower That Shattered the Stone*. Windstar WR-5-3334-4, 1990, Cassette Tape.

———. "Sunshine on My Shoulders." *Poems, Prayers, and Promises*. RCA LSP-4499, 1971, Long Playing Record.

———. "Sweet Surrender." *Back Home Again*. RCA CPL1-0548, 1974, Long Playing Record.

———. "Sweet, Sweet Life." *Whose Garden Was This*. RCA LSP-4414, 1970, Long Playing Record.

———. "Take Me Home, Country Roads." *Poems, Prayers, and Promises*. RCA LSP-4499, 1971, Long Playing Record.

———. "Take Me to Tomorrow." *Take Me to Tomorrow*. RCA LSP-4278,970, Long Playing Record.

———. "Thanks to You." *The Flower That Shattered the Stone*. Windstar WR-5-3334-4, 1990, Cassette Tape.

———. "This Old Guitar." *Back Home Again*. RCA CPL1-0548, 1974, Long Playing Record.

———. "Thought of You." *It's About Time*. RCA AFL1-4683, 1983, Long Playing Record.

———. "Tools." *Aerie*. RCA LSP-4607, 1971, Long Playing Record.

———. "To the Wild Country." *I Want to Live*. RCA AFL1-2521, 1977, Long Playing Record.

———. "Tradewinds." *I Want to Live*. RCA AFL1-2521, 1977, Long Playing Record.

———. "True Love Takes Time." *One World*. RCA AFL1-5811, 1986, Long Playing Record.

———. "Two Different Directions." *Different Directions*. Windstar WR-58888-4, 1991, Cassette Tape.

———. "Two Shots." *Windsong*. RCA APL1-1183, 1975, Long Playing Record.

———. "What One Man Can Do." *Seasons of the Heart*. RCA AFL1-4256, 1981-1982, Long Playing Record.

———. "What's on Your Mind." *J.D. (John Denver)*. RCA AQL1-3075, 1979, Long Playing Record.

———. "Whiskey Basin Blues." *Farewell Andromeda*. RCA APL1-0101, 1973, Long Playing Record.

———. "Whispering Jessie." *Higher Ground*. Windstar D4-72850, 1988, Cassette Tape.

———. "Wild Montana Skies." *It's About Time*. RCA AFL1-4683, 1983, Long Playing Record.

———. "Windsong." *Windsong*. RCA APL1-1183, 1975, Long Playing Record.

———. "Wooden Indian." *Poems, Prayers, and Promises*. RCA LSP-4499, 1971, Long Playing Record.

———. "World Game." *It's About Time*. RCA AFL1-4683, 1983, Long Playing Record.

———. "Wrangell Mountain Song." *Spirit*. RCA APL1-1694, 1976, Long Playing Record.

———. "You're So Beautiful." *J.D. (John Denver)*. RCA AQL1-3075, 1979, Long Playing Record.

———. "Zachary and Jennifer." *Farewell Andromeda*. RCA APL1-0101, 1973, Long Playing Record.

O'Day, Gail R., and David Peterson, eds. *The Access Bible: New Revised Standard Version with the Apocryphal/Deuterocanonical Books*. New York: Oxford University Press, 1999.

Okun, Milton, ed. *John Denver Anthology*. Chester, NY: Cherry Lane Music, 1982.

Album, Year of Release, and Songs by John Denver

The albums and the year of release for each are listed in alphabetical order with the songs referred to in this book.

Aerie (1972)
> Starwood in Aspen
> 60 Second Song for a Bank, with the Phrase
>> "May We Help You Today?"
> All of My Memories
> The Eagle and the Hawk
> Tools

An Evening with John Denver (1975)
> Annie's Other Song

Autograph (1980)
> Dancing with the Mountains
> In My Heart
> American Child
> Autograph

Back Home Again (1974)
> Back Home Again
> Matthew
> The Music Is You
> Annie's Song

ALBUM, YEAR OF RELEASE, AND SONGS BY JOHN DENVER

Cool an' Green an' Shady
Eclipse
Sweet Surrender
This Old Guitar

Different Directions (1991)
The Foxfire Suite
Two Different Directions
Amazon (Let This Be a Voice)

Dreamland Express (1985)
Dreamland Express
The Harder They Fall
A Wild Heart Looking for a Home
African Sunrise

Earth Songs (1990)
Earth Day Every Day (Celebrate)

Farewell Andromeda (1973)
I'd Rather Be a Cowboy (Lady's Chains)
Rocky Mountain Suite (Cold Nights in Canada)
Whiskey Basin Blues
Zachary and Jennifer
Farewell Andromeda (Welcome to My Morning)

The Flower that Shattered the Stone (1990)
Thanks to You
Eagles and Horses (I'm Flying Again)
Raven's Child
Ancient Rhymes
The Gift You Are
Stonehaven Sunset

Higher Ground (1988)
Higher Ground
Whispering Jessie
Never a Doubt
Deal with the Ladies
Sing Australia

A Country Girl in Paris
For You
All This Joy
Falling Leaves (The Refugees)
Alaska and Me

It's About Time (1983)
Hold on Tightly
Thought of You
Somethin' About
On the Wings of a Dream
Flight (The Higher We Fly)
Falling out of Love
I Remember Romance
Wild Montana Skies
World Game
It's About Time

I Want to Live (1977)
How Can I Leave You Again
Tradewinds
It Amazes Me
To the Wild Country
Singing Skies and Dancing Waters
I Want to Live
Druthers

J.D. (John Denver) (1979)
Downhill Stuff
What's on Your Mind
Joseph and Joe
Life Is So Good
You're So Beautiful
Songs of . . .

John Denver's Greatest Hits: Volume 3 (1984)
The Gold and Beyond

One World (1986)
Love Is the Master

Love Again
Hey There, Mr. Lonely Heart
Let Us Begin (What Are We Making Weapons for?)
Flying for Me
I Can't Escape
True Love Takes Time
One World
It's a Possibility

Poems, Prayers and Promises (1971)
Poems, Prayers, and Promises
My Sweet Lady
Wooden Indian
Take Me Home, Country Roads
Sunshine on My Shoulders
Around and Around

Rocky Mountain High (1972)
Rocky Mountain High
For Baby (For Bobbie)
Prisoners (Hard Life, Hard Times)
Goodbye Again
Season Suite
   Summer
   Fall
   Winter
   Spring

Rhymes and Reasons (1969)
Daydream
Circus
Rhymes and Reasons
Leaving on a Jet Plane

Some Days Are Diamonds (1981)
Some Days Are Diamonds (Some Days Are Stone)
Sleepin' Alone
Country Love

Seasons of the Heart (1982)
  Seasons of the Heart
  Opposite Tables
  What One Man Can Do
  Shanghai Breezes
  Islands
  Heart to Heart
  Perhaps Love
  Children of the Universe

Spirit (1976)
  Come and Let Me Look in Your Eyes
  Wrangell Mountain Song
  Hitchhiker
  It Makes Me Giggle
  Like a Sad Song

Take Me to Tomorrow (1970)
  Take Me to Tomorrow
  Isabel
  Follow Me
  Aspenglow
  Anthem-Revelation
  Sticky Summer Weather

Whose Garden Was This (1970)
  Sail Away Home
  I Wish I Could Have Been There (Woodstock)
  The Game Is Over
  Sweet, Sweet Life

Windsong (1975)
  Windsong
  Spirit
  Looking for Space
  Love Is Everywhere
  Two Shots
  I'm Sorry
  Fly Away
  Calypso
  Song of Wyoming

John Denver Albums
Chronologically

SPIRIT: This fifteen-foot tall statue of John Denver, titled "Spirit," was erected on the Windstar property in Old Snowmass in 2002. After the property was sold in 2013, the statue was donated to the Colorado Music Hall of Fame at Red Rocks Amphitheater, Morrison, Colorado, ten miles west of Denver. It was installed there in 2015. John Denver was the first inductee to the hall of fame. The statue's name, "Spirit," echoes his 1976 album of the same name and depicts Denver's "The Eagle and the Hawk" on the 1971 Aerie album.

With the Mitchell Trio:

>> *That's the Way It's Gonna Be* (1965)
>> *Violets of Dawn* (1965)
>> *Alive* (1967)
>> *Beginnings: John Denver with the Mitchell Trio* (1974)

John Denver Sings (1966)
Rhymes and Reasons (1969)
Take Me to Tomorrow (1970)
Whose Garden Was This (1970)
Poems, Prayers, and Promises (1971)
Aerie (1971)
Rocky Mountain High (1972)
Farewell Andromeda (1973)
John Denver's Greatest Hits (1973)
Back Home Again (1974)
Windsong (1975)
An Evening with John Denver (1975)
Rocky Mountain Christmas (1975)
Spirit (1976)
Live in London (1976)
I Want to Live (1977)
John Denver's Greatest Hits: Volume 2 (1977)
J.D. (John Denver) (1979)
A Christmas Together (1979)
Autograph (1980)
Some Days Are Diamonds (1981)
Perhaps Love (1981)
Seasons of the Heart (1982)
Rocky Mountain Holiday (1982)
It's About Time (1983)
John Denver's Greatest Hits: Volume 3 (1984)
Dreamland Express (1985)
One World (1986)
Higher Ground (1988)
Earth Songs (1990)
The Flower that Shattered the Stone (1990)
Christmas, Like a Lullaby (1990)

Different Directions (1991)

Take Me Home, Country Roads, and Other Hits (1991)

The Very Best of John Denver (1994)

The Wildlife Concert (1995)

The Rocky Mountain Collection (1996)

Reflections: Songs of Love and Life (1996)

All Aboard! (1997)

Country Roads Collection (1997)

A Celebration of Life (1943–1997) (1997)

The Best of John Denver Live (1997)

The Best of John Denver (1998)

Greatest Country Hits (1998)

Forever, John (1998)

Live at the Sydney Opera House (1999)

Christmas (1999)

Christmas in Concert (2001)

The Harbor Lights Concert (2002)

Songs for America (2002)

The Essential John Denver (2004)

Definitive All-Time Greatest Hits (2004)

16 Biggest Hits (2006)

Live in the U.S.S.R. (2007)

The Essential John Denver (2007)

Playlist: The Very Best of John Denver (2008)

Live at Cedar Rapids (2010)

The Ultimate Collection (2011)

The Classic Christmas Album (2012)

All of My Memories: The John Denver Collection (2014)

Made in the USA
Monee, IL
16 December 2023

49492408R00075